STUDY PLANNER

CHAPTER 01 인칭대명사와 동사	학습일	
UNIT 01	월	일
UNIT 02	월	일
UNIT 03	월	일
UNIT 04	월	일
Review Test	월	일

CHAPTER 02 명사, 관사, 대명사	학습일	
UNIT 05	월	일
UNIT 06	월	일
UNIT 07	월	일
Review Test	월	일

CHAPTER 03 시제	학습일	
UNIT 08	월	일
UNIT 09	월	일
UNIT 10	월	일
Review Test	월	일

CHAPTER 04 조동사	학습일	
UNIT 11	월	일
UNIT 12	월	일
UNIT 13	월	일
Review Test	월	일

CHAPTER 05 문장의 변환	학습일	
UNIT 14	월	일
UNIT 15	월	일
UNIT 16	월	일
UNIT 17	월	일
Review Test	월	일

CHAPTER 06 형용사와 부사	학습일	
UNIT 18	월	일
UNIT 19	월	일
Review Test	월	일

CHAPTER 07 비교 구문	학습일	
UNIT 20	월	일
UNIT 21	월	일
UNIT 22	월	일
Review Test	월	일

CHAPTER 08 to부정사	학습일	
UNIT 23	월	일
UNIT 24	월	일
Review Test	월	일

CHAPTER 09 동명사	학습일	
UNIT 25	월	일
UNIT 26	월	일
Review Test	월	일

CHAPTER 10 문장의 형식	학습일	
UNIT 27	월	일
UNIT 28	월	일
Review Test	월	일

CHAPTER 11 전치사와 접속사	학습일	
UNIT 29	월	일
UNIT 30	월	일
Review Test	월	일

SCORECARD

CHAPTER 01 인칭대명사와 동사	점수	PASS
UNIT 01	/ 35점	30점
UNIT 02	/ 30점	26점
UNIT 03	/ 35점	30점
UNIT 04	/ 35점	30점
Review Test	/ 70점	60점

CHAPTER 02 명사, 관사, 대명사	점수	PASS
UNIT 05	/ 35점	30점
UNIT 06	/ 35점	30점
UNIT 07	/ 35점	30점
Review Test	/ 80점	68점

CHAPTER 03 시제	점수	PASS
UNIT 08	/ 35점	30점
UNIT 09	/ 25점	22점
UNIT 10	/ 30점	26점
Review Test	/ 80점	68점

CHAPTER 04 조동사	점수	PASS
UNIT 11	/ 30점	26점
UNIT 12	/ 30점	26점
UNIT 13	/ 25점	22점
Review Test	/ 80점	68점

CHAPTER 05 문장의 변환	점수	PASS
UNIT 14	/ 30점	26점
UNIT 15	/ 25점	22점
UNIT 16	/ 35점	30점
UNIT 17	/ 25점	22점
Review Test	/ 70점	60점

CHAPTER 06 형용사와 부사	점수	PASS
UNIT 18	/ 30점	26점
UNIT 19	/ 30점	26점
Review Test	/ 60점	51점

CHAPTER 07 비교 구문	점수	PASS
UNIT 20	/ 30점	26점
UNIT 21	/ 30점	26점
UNIT 22	/ 30점	26점
Review Test	/ 80점	68점

CHAPTER 08 to부정사	점수	PASS
UNIT 23	/ 30점	26점
UNIT 24	/ 25점	22점
Review Test	/ 60점	51점

CHAPTER 09 동명사	점수	PASS
UNIT 25	/ 35점	30점
UNIT 26	/ 35점	30점
Review Test	/ 60점	51점

CHAPTER 10 문장의 형식	점수	PASS
UNIT 27	/ 30점	26점
UNIT 28	/ 30점	26점
Review Test	/ 60점	51점

CHAPTER 11 전치사와 접속사	점수	PASS
UNIT 29	/ 30점	26점
UNIT 30	/ 35점	30점
Review Test	/ 60점	51점

내신공략
중학영문법

개념이해책
1

내_신공_략 중학영문법의 구성 및 특징

시리즈 구성

내신공략 중학영문법 시리즈는 중학교 영어 교과과정의 문법 사항을 3레벨로 나누어 수록하고 있으며, 각각의 레벨은 **개념이해책**과 **문제풀이책**으로 구성됩니다. 두 책을 병행하여 학습하는 것이 가장 이상적인 학습법이지만, 교사와 학생의 필요에 따라 둘 중 하나만을 독립적으로도 사용할 수 있도록 구성했습니다.

개념이해책은 문법 개념에 대한 핵심적인 설명과 필수 연습문제로 이루어져 있습니다.

문제풀이책은 각 문법 개념에 대해 총 3단계의 테스트를 통해 체계적으로 문제를 풀어볼 수 있도록 구성되어 있습니다.

특징

❶ 최신 내신 출제 경향 100% 반영

– 신유형과 고난도 서술형 문제 비중 강화

점점 어려워지는 내신 문제의 최신 경향을 철저히 분석·반영하여 고난도 서술형과 신유형 문제의 비중을 더욱 높였습니다. 이 책으로 학습한 학생들은 어떤 유형의 문제에도 대처할 수 있습니다.

– 영어 지시문 문제 제시

영어로 문제가 출제되는 최신 경향을 반영하여, 일부 문제를 영어 지시문으로 제시했습니다. 문제풀이책의 Level 3 Test는 모두 영어 지시문으로만 제시됩니다.

– 독해 지문 어법 문제 수록(문제풀이책)

독해 지문에서 어법 문제가 출제되는 내신 문제 스타일에 익숙해지도록, 독해 지문과 함께 다양한 어법 문제를 풀어볼 수 있습니다.

❷ 개념이해책과 문제풀이책의 연계 학습

문법 개념 설명과 필수 문제로 구성된 개념이해책으로 문법 개념을 학습한 후, 다양한 문제를 3단계로 풀어보는 문제풀이책으로 복습하며 확실한 학습 효과를 거둘 수 있습니다.

❸ 성취도 평가와 수준별 맞춤형 학습 제안

문제를 풀어보고 나서 점수 기준에 따라 학생의 성취도를 평가할 수 있습니다. 개념이해책에서 Let's Check It Out과 Ready for Exams 점수를 합산한 결과에 따라 문제풀이책의 어느 레벨부터 학습하면 되는지 가이드가 제시됩니다. Review Test에서는 일정 점수 이상을 받아야 다음 챕터로 넘어갈 수 있습니다.

❹ 추가 학습을 위한 다양한 학습자료 제공

다양하게 수업에 활용할 수 있는 교사용 자료가 제공됩니다. 다락원 홈페이지(www.darakwon.co.kr)에서 무료로 다운받으실 수 있습니다.

개념이해책과 문제풀이책 연계 학습법

개념이해책으로 문법 개념 학습

문제풀이책으로 문법 개념을 복습

QR코드를 찍으면 개념이해책 문법 설명이 보여요!

개념이해책 Let's Check It Out과 Ready for Exams 풀고 점수 합산

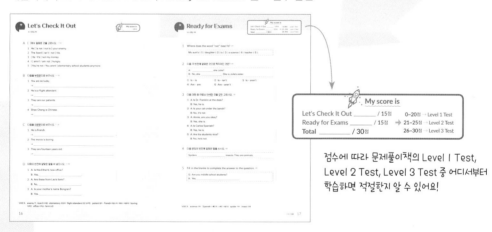

점수에 따라 문제풀이책의 Level 1 Test, Level 2 Test, Level 3 Test 중 어디서부터 학습하면 적절한지 알 수 있어요!

챕터 내용을 모두 학습한 후 Review Test 풀기

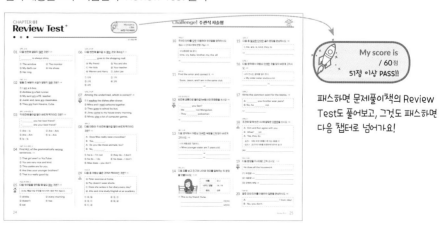

패스하면 문제풀이책의 Review Test도 풀어보고, 그것도 패스하면 다음 챕터로 넘어가요!

개념이해책의 구성

문법 개념 설명

문법 항목에 대한 핵심 내용이 개념(Concept)별로 간결하게 정리되어 있습니다. 표와 도식을 통해 내용을 한눈에 파악하기 쉽습니다.

● Grammar Point
학생들이 잘 모르는 중요한 내용을 꼼꼼하게 짚고 넘어갈 수 있습니다.

● VOCA
예문에 쓰인 주요 단어가 정리되어 편리하며, 문법과 단어 공부를 같이 할 수 있습니다.

Let's Check It Out

Ready for Exams

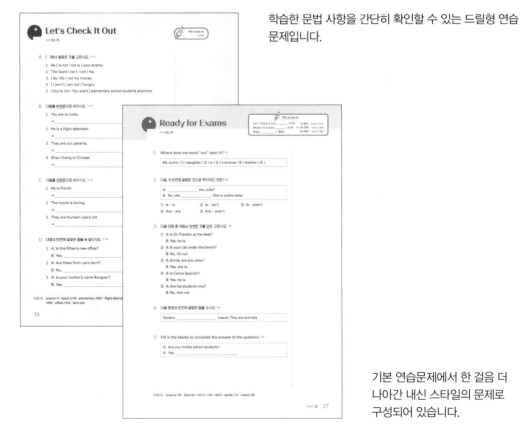

학습한 문법 사항을 간단히 확인할 수 있는 드릴형 연습 문제입니다.

기본 연습문제에서 한 걸음 더 나아간 내신 스타일의 문제로 구성되어 있습니다.

Review Test

챕터 학습이 끝나면 내신 시험 유형의 문제를 풀어보며 배운 내용을 정리합니다. 챕터 내 여러 유닛의 내용을 통합적으로 구성한 문제를 통해 응용력과 실전 감각을 키울 수 있습니다.

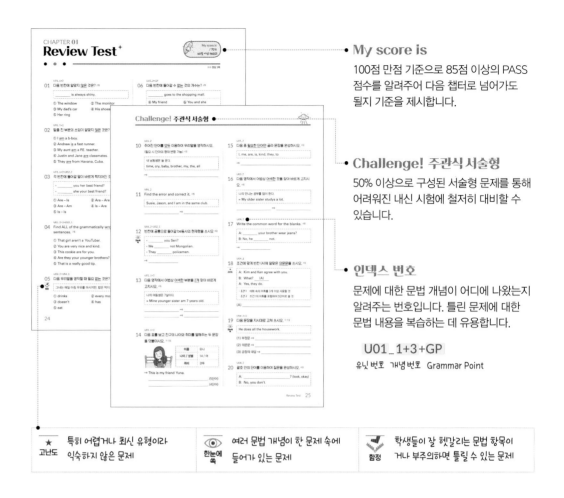

My score is

100점 만점 기준으로 85점 이상의 PASS 점수를 알려주어 다음 챕터로 넘어가도 될지 기준을 제시합니다.

Challenge! 주관식 서술형

50% 이상으로 구성된 서술형 문제를 통해 어려워진 내신 시험에 철저히 대비할 수 있습니다.

인덱스 번호

문제에 대한 문법 개념이 어디에 나왔는지 알려주는 번호입니다. 틀린 문제에 대한 문법 내용을 복습하는 데 유용합니다.

U01_1+3+GP

유닛 번호 개념번호 Grammar Point

★ 고난도	특히 어렵거나 최신 유형이라 익숙하지 않은 문제
👁 한눈에 쏙	여러 문법 개념이 한 문제 속에 들어가 있는 문제
✅ 함정	학생들이 잘 헷갈리는 문법 항목이거나 부주의하면 틀릴 수 있는 문제

시험 직전에 챙겨 보는 비법 노트

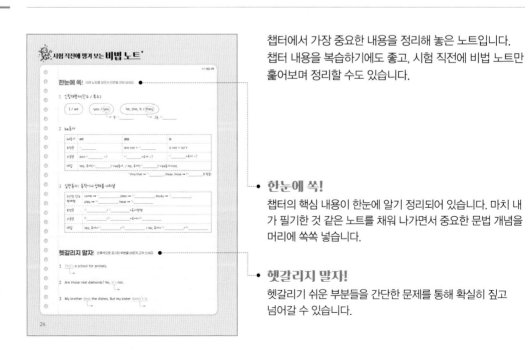

챕터에서 가장 중요한 내용을 정리해 놓은 노트입니다. 챕터 내용을 복습하기에도 좋고, 시험 직전에 비법 노트만 훑어보며 정리할 수도 있습니다.

한눈에 쏙!

챕터의 핵심 내용이 한눈에 알기 정리되어 있습니다. 마치 내가 필기한 것 같은 노트를 채워 나가면서 중요한 문법 개념을 머리에 쏙쏙 넣습니다.

헷갈리지 말자!

헷갈리기 쉬운 부분들을 간단한 문제를 통해 확실히 짚고 넘어갈 수 있습니다.

차례

틀에 박힌 예문이 아니라, 학생의 생각을 살리는 예문. 틀에 박힌 문제가 아니라, 한 번 더 생각하게 하는 참신한 문제. 다양하고 새로운 유형의 문제와 예문들은 내공 중학영문법 출시 이후 줄곧 수업 교재로 채택하고 있는 이유입니다. 최근 학교 내신 시험에서도 내공과 비슷한 유형의 문제가 출제되는 걸 보면, 교재의 이름처럼 정말 대단한 내공을 가진 문법서입니다.

창원 쥬기스영어교실 원장 **이연홍**

다년간 예비중을 위한 문법 특강을 하면서 이번에 바꾸게 된 다락원 내신공략 중학영문법은 짧은 시간에 기초를 다질 수 있도록 중요 설명과 다양한 문제를 풀 수 있어 단시간에 실력 향상을 할 수 있어 학생들 모두 만족한 수업을 했습니다.

오창 로제타스톤영어학원 원장 **강보민**

평소 문법 수업에서 '아이들이 잘 이해하고 있는가'를 확인하는 것에 중점을 두는데 내공 중학영문법의 교재 구성이 이 부분에 많은 도움이 되었습니다. 개념 부분의 빈칸 문제와 두 권에 걸쳐 연습해 볼 수 있는 활용 문제들이 개념 정립과 문제 응용까지 확실하게 잡아줘서 좋았어요. 수업과 과제, 단어, 테스트까지 교재만으로도 충분히 전반적인 문법 커리큘럼을 구성할 수 있었습니다.

전주 퍼플영어학원 원장 **이서원**

다양한 유형과 풍부한 문제 풀이로 중학 기본 문법에 완벽히 대비할 수 있었다. 또한 학생들의 눈높이에 맞춘 예문들에 쉽고 정확하게 이해할 수 있는 책으로 적극 추천한다.

전남무안 이써밋영수학원 원장 **김지현**

정확하고 자세한 설명과 실제 사용할 수 있는 생생한 예문들이 많아서 좋았다. 다양한 연습 문제와 체계적인 구성들로 문법 실력에 향상을 보였다.

전남목포 홍일고 **양재동**

중학 내신에 꼭 필요한 핵심적인 문법들을 학생들이 이해하기 쉽게 설명해주고 있다. 자기 주도 학습에도 충분히 활용하게끔 문법 설명과 문제가 적절히 구성되어 있다. 탄탄한 영어 실력을 위한 영문법 책이다.

충북 청주 해피써니영어 원장 이선미

개념이해책과 문제풀이책에 있는 Fail 컷으로 공부했더니 모든 문제를 푸는 데에 있어 꼼꼼히 푸는 습관이 생겼고, 대부분 한눈에 보기 쉬운 표로 구성되어 있어 이해하기 쉬웠다. 어렵기만 하던 문법이 지금은 나의 무기가 되었다.

충북 청주 일신여고 2학년 신채은

기본부터 고난도 문제들까지 꼼꼼하게 다뤄주어서 좋다. 뻔하지 않는 다양한 문제유형과 학생들의 실책 포인트를 잘 챙겨줘서 여러 책 보지 않아도 실속 있게 챙겨주는 너무 든든한 책이다.

김포 MDS영어 원장 정지윤

외고 목표로 공부 중이다. 중1 때 만나게 된 책인데, 다양한 문제들로 실력이 향상되는 것을 느낀다. 빈칸 채우기를 하면서 개념 복습도 가능하고 나의 부족한 점을 직접 확인할 수 있어서 좋다.

학생 장예원, 한지우

미국 가서 7학년 때 처음으로 미국에서 문법을 배웠는데 내공 책으로 공부한 덕분에 문법이 쉬웠다. 8학년 때는 미국 native 현지인 학생들이 오히려 문법 부분에서 많이 어려워했는데 한국 유학생인 내가 오히려 내공 책 덕분에 좋은 점수를 받을 수 있었다.

Chaminade College Preparatory School 8학년 황인태

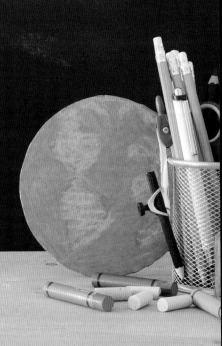

CHAPTER 01
인칭대명사와 동사

UNIT 01 인칭대명사와 be동사

CONCEPT 1 인칭대명사

인칭대명사는 사람 또는 사물을 대신 가리키는 말로, 인칭·수·격에 따라 다음과 같이 변한다.

격	단수				복수			
	주격	소유격	목적격	소유대명사	주격	소유격	목적격	소유대명사
1인칭	I	my	me	mine	we	our	us	ours
2인칭	you	your	you	yours	you	your	you	yours
3인칭	he	his	him	his	they	their	them	theirs
	she	her	her	hers				
	it	its	it					

She is my cousin. She is smart.

I have a brother. His name is Kim Junil.

This is my new phone. It is mine.

We have two dogs. They are lovely.

CONCEPT 2 be동사의 의미와 현재형

be동사는 '~이다, (~에) 있다'의 의미이고 주어에 따라 am, are, is로 변화한다.

주어	be동사
I	am
you, we, they	are
he, she, it, this, that	is

I am very smart.　　　　You are stupid.

He is in Cheongdam-dong.　　　　They are figure skaters.

CONCEPT 3 be동사의 줄임말

be동사는 '(apostrophe)를 사용하여 주어와 줄여 쓸 수 있다.

주어	be동사	줄임말
I	am	I'm
you, we, they	are	you're, we're, they're
he, she, it, this, that	is	he's, she's, it's, that's

I'm so cool.　　　　You're very attractive.

She's from Jamaica.　　　　They're in the stadium.

GRAMMAR POINT

주격, 소유격, 목적격의 해석

● 주격: ~은/는/이/가

● 소유격: ~의

● 목적격: ~을/를/에게

● 소유대명사: ~의 것

인칭대명사

● you는 단수(너)와 복수(너희들)를 모두 가리킬 수 있다.

● they는 사람(그들)과 사물(그것들)을 모두 가리킬 수 있다.

you and your sister → you
those children → they
these tables → they
Maria and David → they

● 고유명사의 소유격은 -'s로 표현한다.

Ted → Ted's

줄여 쓸 수 없는 경우

● This is는 줄여서 쓰지 않는다.

● 고유명사와 be동사는 줄여서 쓰지 않는다.

Ted, ~~this's~~ (→ this is) my grandmother.

(Ted, 이분은 나의 할머니이셔.)

~~Andy's~~ (→ Andy is) in the living room.

(Andy는 거실에 있어.)

VOCA　cousin 사촌 | smart 똑똑한 | lovely 사랑스러운 | stupid 멍청한 | figure skater 피겨 스케이트 선수 | cool 멋진 | attractive 매력적인 | Jamaica 자메이카 | stadium 경기장 | living room 거실

Let's Check It Out

My score is
/ 25점

A 다음 표의 빈칸에 알맞은 말을 쓰시오. 각 1점

	주격	소유격	목적격	소유대명사
1	I	my	me	
2	she	her		hers
3	you		you	yours
4	it	its		
5	Andy		Andy	Andy's

B [ ]에서 알맞은 것을 고르시오. 각 1점

1 I [is / am] very strong.

2 You [is / are] special.

3 She [is / are] a game developer.

4 They [is / are] truck drivers.

5 Lou [is / are] a very good singer.

C 빈칸에 알맞은 be동사를 쓰시오. 각 1점

1 I _____ a genius.

2 It _____ her new schoolbag.

3 My car _____ very expensive.

4 These pictures _____ very nice.

5 The kids _____ in the garden.

D 다음 표의 빈칸에 알맞은 말을 써 넣으시오. (줄여 쓸 수 없는 경우 ×로 표시할 것) 각 1점

	주어	be동사	줄임말
1	I		I'm
2	you	are	
3	he		he's
4	she	is	
5	it		
6	we		we're
7	they	are	
8	this	is	
9	Lucy		
10	Tony and Gina		

VOCA special 특별한 | game developer 게임 개발자 | genius 천재 | schoolbag 책가방

Ready for Exams

>>> 정답 2쪽

My score is		
Let's Check It Out _____ / 25점	0~24점 → Level 1 Test	
Ready for Exams _____ / 10점	25~29점 → Level 2 Test	
Total _____ / 35점	30~35점 → Level 3 Test	

1 각 빈칸에 들어갈 말이 순서대로 나열된 것은? 2점

- It _____ her pet snake.
- My dog _____ four years old.
- His glasses _____ pink.

① is – is – is   ② is – am – are   ③ is – is – are

④ are – is – is   ⑤ am – are – are

2 빈칸에 들어갈 be동사의 현재형이 나머지와 <u>다른</u> 것은? 2점

① He _____ a good teacher.

② The flower _____ beautiful.

③ The cat _____ under the table.

④ Chris _____ from Vancouver, Canada.

⑤ Yuna and Mimi _____ best friends.

3 Which sentence is grammatically wrong? 2점

① You're my sunshine.

② I'm a middle school student.

③ She's from Yanbian.

④ This's a KTX for Busan.

⑤ Charles is my only friend.

4 Look at the picture and complete the sentence according to the condition. 4점

그의 아이들은 지금 해변에 있다.

· 어휘   he, kids

· 조건 1   필요하면 인칭대명사의 격을 변화할 것

· 조건 2   be동사의 현재형을 쓸 것

→ _____ _____ _____ at the _____ now.

VOCA   pet 반려동물 | snake 뱀 | glasses 안경 | Vancouver 밴쿠버(캐나다 서부의 항구 도시) | sunshine 햇빛, 행복 | Yanbian
연변(조선족 비중이 높은, 중국 길림성 동부에 있는 자치주)

UNIT

02 be동사의 부정문과 의문문

1 be동사의 부정문

be동사 뒤에 not을 붙여 만들며 '～이 아니다, (～에) 있지 않다'의 의미로 사용된다. 줄여서 사용하기도 한다.

주어		주어＋be동사＋not	줄임말
단수	1인칭	I am not	I'm not
	2인칭	you are not	you're not 또는 you aren't
	3인칭	he is not she is not it is not	he/she/it isn't he's/she's/it's not
복수	1인칭	we are not	we're not 또는 we aren't
	2인칭	you are not	you're not 또는 you aren't
	3인칭	they are not	they're not 또는 they aren't

You are not alone.

We're not in the kitchen.

He isn't my boyfriend anymore.

GRAMMAR POINT

줄여 쓰지 않는 말

• am not은 줄여 쓰지 않는다.

• I ~~amn't~~ (→ am not) a professor.

2 be동사의 의문문과 대답

be동사의 의문문은 be동사를 주어 앞에 쓰고 마지막에 물음표(?)를 쓴다. 이에 대한 긍정의 대답은 「Yes, 주어＋be동사.」로, 부정의 대답은 「No, 주어＋be동사＋not.」으로 한다.

be동사의 의문문	대답	
주어＋be동사 ～. → Be동사＋주어 ～?	긍정	Yes, 주어＋be동사.
	부정	No, 주어＋be동사＋not.

The gallery is open today.

→ Is the gallery open today?

   – Yes, it is. / No, it's not.[No, it isn't.]

They are soccer players.

→ Are they soccer players?

   – Yes, they are. / No, they aren't.[No, they're not.]

대답에서 대명사 사용

• 대답에서는 주어를 대명사로 쓴다.

  Is Simon a rapper?

  – Yes, he is. / No, he's not.

• this와 that은 it으로, these와 those는 they로 답한다.

  Is this your pen?

  – Yes, it is. / No, it's not.

  Are those from your garden?

  – Yes, they are. / No, they aren't.

VOCA　alone 혼자 | not ～ anymore 더 이상 ～ 않다 | gallery 미술관 | open 문을 연 | professor 교수 | rapper 래퍼

A [ ]에서 알맞은 것을 고르시오. 각 1점

1 He [is not / not is] your enemy.

2 The lizard [isn't / not] his.

3 [Its / It's] not my money.

4 I [amn't / am not] hungry.

5 [You're not / You arent] elementary school students anymore.

B 다음을 <u>부정문</u>으로 바꾸시오. 각 1점

1 You are so lucky.

→ _____

2 He is a flight attendant.

→ _____

3 They are our patients.

→ _____

4 Shao Cheng is Chinese.

→ _____

C 다음을 <u>의문문</u>으로 바꾸시오. 각 1점

1 He is French.

→ _____

2 The movie is boring.

→ _____

3 They are fourteen years old.

→ _____

D 대화의 빈칸에 알맞은 말을 써 넣으시오. 각 1점

1 A: Is this Ethan's new office?

B: Yes, _____ _____.

2 A: Are these from Leo's farm?

B: No, _____ _____.

3 A: Is your mother's name Bongran?

B: Yes, _____ _____.

VOCA enemy 적 | lizard 도마뱀 | elementary 초등의 | flight attendant 항공 승무원 | patient 환자 | French 프랑스의; 프랑스 사람(의) | boring 지루한 | office 사무실 | farm 농장

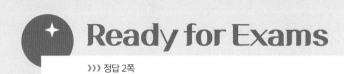

>>> 정답 2쪽

1 Where does the word "not" best fit? 2점

> My aunt's (①) daughter (②) is (③) a science (④) teacher (⑤).

2 다음 각 빈칸에 알맞은 것으로 짝지어진 것은? 2점

> A: _____ she Julie?
> B: No, she _____ . She is Julie's sister.

① Is – is   ② Is – isn't   ③ Is – aren't

④ Are – are   ⑤ Are – aren't

3 다음 대화 중 어법상 <u>어색한</u> 것을 <u>모두</u> 고르시오. 3점

① A: Is Dr. Franklin at the desk?
   B: Yes, he is.
② A: Is your cat under the bench?
   B: No, it's not.
③ A: Annie, are you okay?
   B: Yes, she is.
④ A: Is Carlos Spanish?
   B: Yes, he is.
⑤ A: Are his students nice?
   B: No, he's not.

4 다음 문장의 빈칸에 알맞은 말을 쓰시오. 4점

> Spiders _____ insects. They are animals.

5 Fill in the blanks to complete the answer to the question. 4점

> Q: Are you middle school students?
> A: Yes, _____ _____ .

VOCA science 과학 | Spanish 스페인의; 스페인 사람(의) | spider 거미 | insect 곤충

UNIT
03 일반동사

1 일반동사의 의미와 종류

일반동사는 be동사와 조동사를 제외하고 '~하다'로 해석되는 말이다. 주어의 동작이나 상태를 나타낸다.

동작	go, come, sit, walk, run, eat...
상태	have, like, love, think...

I go to school by bus.

They only eat healthy food.

I have long hair.

You like her so much.

2 일반동사의 3인칭 단수 현재형

주어가 3인칭 단수이고 시제가 현재일 때 동사원형에 -s나 -es를 붙인다.

대부분의 동사	+ -s	come → comes, walk → walks, eat → eats, sing → sings, run → runs
-s, -x, -sh, -ch, -o로 끝나는 동사	+ -es	pass → passes, wash → washes, mix → mixes, teach → teaches, do → does
'자음+y'로 끝나는 동사	-y → -ies	study → studies, fly → flies, cry → cries, try → tries
have		has

She plays soccer with her kids.

My sister mixes juice and coke together.

The airplane flies fast.

Their uncle has an expensive yacht.

GRAMMAR POINT

조동사
- 동사를 보조해 주는 동사: can(~할 수 있다), will(~할 것이다) 등
  You can do it! (너는 할 수 있어!)
  I will go there. (나는 거기에 갈 것이다.)

3인칭 단수
- 1인칭(I)이나 2인칭(you)을 제외하고 하나만 가리키는 모든 말
  he, she, it, her sister, my brother, their car, John, Korea, a desk...

'모음+y'로 끝나는 동사
- '모음+y'는 -s만 붙인다.
  play → plays
  pay → pays
  stay → stays
  say → says

VOCA healthy 건강에 좋은 | hair 머리(카락) | pass 통과하다 | mix 섞다 | try 노력하다 | coke 콜라 | expensive 비싼 | yacht 요트 | stay 머무르다

18

Let's Check It Out

A 빈칸에 알맞은 단어를 [보기]에서 골라 쓰시오. 각 1점

| 보기 | watch | wear | play | eat |

1 The boys _____ badminton.

2 Some baseball players _____ sunglasses.

3 People _____ a lot of YouTube.

4 I _____ Shooting Star ice cream every day.

B 다음 표의 빈칸에 알맞은 말을 써 넣으시오. 각 1점

	일반동사	3인칭 단수 현재형
1	come	
2	run	
3	catch	
4	go	
5	pass	
6	wash	
7	do	
8	study	
9	fly	
10	fix	
11	grow	
12	enjoy	
13	dance	
14	have	

C 괄호 안의 동사를 빈칸에 알맞게 현재형으로 쓰시오. 각 1점

1 I _____ up at six in the morning. (get)

2 My brother _____ a new cell phone. (have)

3 Her baby _____ every night. (cry)

4 Many people _____ KakaoTalk games. (play)

5 Ian and John _____ their homework together. (do)

VOCA wear 입다, 신다, 쓰다 | a lot of 많은 | shooting star 유성, 별똥별 | cell phone 휴대폰 | do one's homework 숙제를 하다

Ready for Exams

1 빈칸에 알맞은 동사의 현재형이 나머지와 <u>다른</u> 것은? 2점

① Tom and John _____ soccer.

② They _____ the game.

③ We _____ on the playground.

④ My friends _____ *baduk*.

⑤ Yuna and Mina _____ the dishes.

2 다음 각 빈칸에 들어갈 말이 순서대로 나열된 것은? 2점

> • We _____ school uniforms.
> • They _____ frogs with their hands.
> • She _____ next to me.

① wears – catch – sits   ② play – catches – sit   ③ wear – catch – sits

④ play – do – sit   ⑤ wear – does – sit

3 How many sentences are grammatically <u>wrong</u>? 2점

> ⓐ We like scary stories.
> ⓑ My grandma get up early every morning.
> ⓒ Her dad work for a bank.
> ⓓ Jisu goes to school on foot.
> ⓔ My sister dances cha-cha.

① 0개   ② 1개   ③ 2개

④ 3개   ⑤ 4개

4 다음 문장을 주어진 주어로 바꾸어 쓰시오. 3점

> The guests stay at the hotel tonight.

→ The guest _____.

5 Write the common word for the blanks. 3점

> • He _____ blue eyes.
> • My sister _____ salad for lunch.

→ _____

VOCA playground 운동장, 놀이터 | *baduk* 바둑 | school uniform 교복 | next to ~의 옆에 | scary 무서운 | on foot 걸어서 | cha-cha
차차차(라틴 아메리카의 빠른 춤)

UNIT 04 일반동사의 부정문과 의문문

1 일반동사의 부정문

일반동사의 원형 앞에 주어에 따라 **do not[don't]** 또는 **does not[doesn't]**을 쓴다.

3인칭 단수 주어	주어+does not[doesn't]+동사원형
그 외 모든 주어	주어+do not[don't]+동사원형

I hate you. → I don't hate you.

My brother likes pizza. → My brother doesn't like pizza.

We eat homemade food. → We don't eat homemade food.

수	인칭	be동사의 부정문	일반동사의 부정문
단수	1	am not	do not[don't]+동사원형
	2	are not[aren't]	do not[don't]+동사원형
	3	is not[isn't]	does not[doesn't]+동사원형
복수	1, 2, 3	are not[aren't]	do not[don't]+동사원형

2 일반동사의 의문문과 대답

주어의 인칭과 수에 따라 **Do**나 **Does**가 문장 앞에 나가고 **Yes/No**로 답한다. 주어가 3인칭 단수일 때만 does를 쓰고, 그 외 모든 주어는 do를 쓴다.

수	인칭	인칭대명사	의문문	대답
단수	1인칭	I	Do I ~?	Yes, you do. / No, you don't.
	2인칭	you	Do you ~?	Yes, I do. / No, I don't.
	3인칭	he/she/it	Does he/she/it ~?	Yes, he/she/it does. No, he/she/it doesn't.
복수	1인칭	we	Do we ~?	Yes, we[you] do. / No, we[you] don't.
	2인칭	you	Do you ~?	Yes, we do. / No, we don't.
	3인칭	they	Do they ~?	Yes, they do. / No, they don't.

You love each other. → Do you love each other? – Yes, we do. / No, we don't.

Tom remembers your birthday. → Does Tom remember your birthday?

– Yes, he does. / No, he doesn't.

They study science. → Do they study science? – Yes, they do. / No, they don't.

GRAMMAR POINT

수와 인칭별 주어의 예

- 1인칭 단수: I
- 2인칭 단수: you
- 3인칭 단수: he, she, it, Tom, my sister...
- 복수(1, 2, 3인칭): we, they, you and I, students...

의문문의 비교

- be동사 의문문: be동사+주어 ~?
- 일반동사 의문문: Do/does+주어+동사원형 ~?

  Is he tired? (그는 피곤하니?)

  Does he know? (그는 알고 있니?)

VOCA homemade 집에서 만든 | each other 서로 | remember 기억하다 | birthday 생일 | tired 피곤한

Let's Check It Out

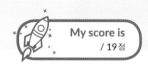

My score is
/ 19점

>>> 정답 3쪽

A [ ]에서 알맞은 것을 고르시오. 각 1점

1 I [don't / doesn't] like sports.

2 She [don't / doesn't] clean her room.

3 [Do / Are] you learn coding at school?

4 [Do / Does] the man answer the phone?

5 [Does / Do] his pet [have / has] red eyes?

B 괄호 안의 단어들을 빈칸에 알맞은 순서로 배열하시오. 각 1점

1 My mom _____ kimchi. (does, make, not)

2 He _____ math. (not, does, teach)

3 I _____ my phone bill. (do, pay, not)

4 You _____ vegetables. (not, do, like)

5 She _____ to school. (not, does, walk)

C 밑줄 친 부분이 어색하면 바르게 고치시오. 각 1점

1 <u>You do listen</u> to K-pop all day long?   ➞ _____

2 <u>Do your dogs take</u> naps?   ➞ _____

3 <u>Does the musical has</u> any funny scenes?   ➞ _____

4 <u>Do her aunt teach</u> Korean?   ➞ _____

D 빈칸에 알맞은 말을 써 넣으시오. 각 1점

1 A: _____ you like to read books?

   B: Yes, _____ _____. I have many storybooks.

2 A: Does your sister study hard?

   B: _____, _____ _____. She plays a lot of games.

3 A: Do you and your sister play the piano?

   B: _____, _____ _____. We play the piano every day.

4 A: Does Alex eat breakfast every morning?

   B: No, _____ _____. He doesn't have time.

5 A: Do they cook well?

   B: _____, _____ _____. Their food isn't delicious.

VOCA coding 코딩 | answer 답하다, (전화를) 받다 | math 수학 | phone bill 전화 요금 (고지서) | vegetable 야채 | all day long 하루 종일 | take a nap 낮잠 자다 | musical 뮤지컬 | funny 우스운 | scene 장면 | Korean 한국어 | storybook 이야기책, 동화책 | delicious 맛있는

22

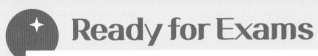

Ready for Exams

1 Which is suitable for the blank? 2점

> We _____ mathematics.

① don't like   ② like don't   ③ likes

④ aren't like   ⑤ like aren't

2 다음 각 빈칸에 들어갈 말이 바르게 연결된 것은? 2점

> • _____ don't have a TV set in the house.
> • _____ don't have any plants in the room.

① I – They   ② I – She   ③ They – She

④ We – She   ⑤ You – He

3 어법상 어색한 것으로 짝지어진 것은? 3점

> ⓐ The boy not busy.
> ⓑ My sister doesn't drink milk.
> ⓒ My grandpa isn't drive a car.
> ⓓ Do your child learn Chinese at home?
> ⓔ Does he watches TV in the living room?

① ⓐ, ⓓ   ② ⓒ, ⓔ   ③ ⓐ, ⓒ, ⓓ

④ ⓒ, ⓓ, ⓔ   ⑤ ⓐ, ⓒ, ⓓ, ⓔ

4 다음 문장을 부정문으로 바꾸어 쓰시오. 4점

> My mother likes grapes.

→ _____ .

5 Find the error and correct it. 5점

> Jack is very lazy. He doesn't exercise. Is he tired? Of course, he is. Does he his homework? No, he doesn't.

_____ → _____

VOCA mathematics 수학 | plant 식물 | Chinese 중국어 | living room 거실 | lazy 게으른 | exercise 운동하다 | tired 피곤한

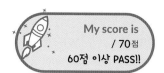

>>> 정답 3쪽

---

01 U01_1+2
다음 빈칸에 알맞지 <u>않은</u> 것은? 2점

> _____ is always shiny.

① The window ② The monitor
③ My dad's car ④ His shoes
⑤ Her ring

02 U01_1+2
밑줄 친 부분의 쓰임이 알맞지 <u>않은</u> 것은? 2점

① I <u>am</u> a b-boy.
② Andrew <u>is</u> a fast runner.
③ My aunt <u>am</u> a P.E. teacher.
④ Justin and Jane <u>are</u> classmates.
⑤ They <u>are</u> from Havana, Cuba.

03 U01_1+2+U02_2
각 빈칸에 들어갈 말이 바르게 짝지어진 것은? 2점

> • _____ you her best friend?
> • _____ she your best friend?

① Are – Is ② Are – Are
③ Are – Am ④ Is – Are
⑤ Is – Is

04 U01_1+2+U02_1
Find ALL of the grammatically <u>wrong</u> sentences. 2점

① That girl aren't a YouTuber.
② You are very nice and kind.
③ This cookie are for you.
④ Are they your younger brothers?
⑤ That is a really good tip.

05 U03_2+U04_1
다음 우리말을 영작할 때 필요 <u>없는</u> 것은? 2점

> 그녀는 매일 아침 우유를 마시지만, 밥은 먹지 않는다.

① drinks ② every morning
③ doesn't ④ has
⑤ eat

---

06 U03_2+GP
다음 빈칸에 들어갈 수 <u>없는</u> 것의 개수는? 2점

> _____ goes to the shopping mall.

ⓐ My friend ⓑ You and she
ⓒ Her kids ⓓ Your teacher
ⓔ Warren and Harry ⓕ John Lee

① 0개 ② 1개
③ 2개 ④ 3개
⑤ 4개

07 U03_2+GP
Among the underlined, which is correct? 2점

한눈에 쏙

① I <u>washes</u> the dishes after dinner.
② Mina and I <u>read</u> cartoons together.
③ They <u>goes</u> to school by bus.
④ Jinsu <u>come</u> to my house every morning.
⑤ Minsu <u>play</u> a lot of computer games.

08 U04_2
다음 대화의 각 빈칸에 들어갈 말이 바르게 짝지어진 것은? 2점

> A: Does Max really raise crocodiles?
> B: Yes, _____.
> A: Do you like those animals, too?
> B: No, _____.

① he is – I'm not ② they do – I don't
③ he do – I do ④ he does – I don't
⑤ Max does – you don't

09 U03_2
다음 중 어법상 옳은 것끼리 짝지어진 것은? 3점

★ 고난도

ⓐ Peter exercise at home.
ⓑ Psy doesn't wear shorts.
ⓒ Does she writes in her diary every day?
ⓓ Jiho and Jina study English at an academy.

① ⓐ, ⓑ ② ⓐ, ⓒ
③ ⓑ, ⓒ ④ ⓑ, ⓓ
⑤ ⓒ, ⓓ

10 U03_2
주어진 단어를 <u>모두</u> 이용하여 우리말을 영작하시오.
(필요 시 단어의 형태 변형 가능) 4점

> 내 남동생은 늘 운다.
> time, cry, baby, brother, my, the, all

→ _____

11 U01_2
Find the error and correct it. 4점

> Susie, Jason, and I am in the same club.

_____ → _____

12 U01_2+U02_1
빈칸에 공통으로 들어갈 be동사의 현재형을 쓰시오 4점

> • _____ you Seri?
> • We _____ not Mongolian.
> • They _____ policemen.

→ _____

13 U01_1+2
다음 영작에서 어법상 <u>어색한</u> 부분을 <u>2개</u> 찾아 바르게 고치시오. 4점

> 나의 여동생은 7살이다.
> = Mine younger sister am 7 years old.

_____ → _____
_____ → _____

14 U01_1+2
다음 표를 보고 친구의 나이와 취미를 말해주는 두 문장을 덧붙이시오. 각 3점

이름	유나
나이 / 성별	14 / 여
취미	권투

→ This is my friend Yuna.

_____. (5단어)
_____. (4단어)

15 U01_2
다음 중 **필요한** 단어만 골라 문장을 완성하시오. 4점

> I, me, are, is, kind, they, to

→ _____

16 U03_2
다음 영작에서 어법상 <u>어색한</u> 것을 찾아 바르게 고치시오. 4점

> 나의 언니는 공부를 많이 한다.
> = My older sister studys a lot.

_____ → _____

17 U04_2
Write the common word for the blanks. 4점

> A: _____ your brother wear jeans?
> B: No, he _____ not.

→ _____

18 U04_2 ★고난도
조건에 맞게 빈칸 (A)에 알맞은 <u>의문문</u>을 쓰시오. 4점

> A: Kim and Ken agree with you.
> B: What?   (A)
> A: Yes, they do.
> ·조건 1 대화 속의 어휘를 3개 이상 사용할 것
> ·조건 2 조건1의 어휘를 포함하여 5단어로 쓸 것

(A) _____

19 U04_1+2
다음 문장을 지시대로 고쳐 쓰시오. 각 3점

> He does all the housework.

(1) 부정문 → _____
(2) 의문문 → _____
(3) 긍정의 대답 → _____

20 U04_2
괄호 안의 단어를 이용하여 질문을 완성하시오. 4점

> A: _____? (look, okay)
> B: No, you don't.

›››› 정답 4쪽

한눈에 쏙! 아래 노트를 보면서 빈칸을 채워 보세요.

1 인칭대명사(단수 / 복수)

I / we   you /you   he, she, it /they

뜻: 1)_____   그들, 2)_____

2 be동사

be동사	am	are	is
부정문	1)_____	are not = 2)_____	is not = isn't
의문문	Am+3)_____ ~?	4)_____+주어 ~?	5)_____+주어 ~?
대답	Yes, 주어(ᵇ)_____)*+be동사. / No, 주어(ᵇ_____)*+be동사+not.		

*this/that → 7)_____, these, those → 8)_____로 받음!

3 일반동사: 동작이나 상태를 나타냄

3인칭 단수 현재형	come → 1)_____, pass → 2)_____, study → 3)_____, play → 4)_____, have → 5)_____
부정문	ᵇ)_____ / 7)_____+동사원형
의문문	8)_____ / 9)_____+주어+10)_____
대답	Yes, 주어+11)_____ / 12)_____. / No, 주어+13)_____ / 14)_____.

헷갈리지 말자! 초록색으로 표시된 부분을 바르게 고쳐 쓰세요.

1 This's a school for animals.

2 Are those real diamonds? – No, it's not.

3 My brother deos the dishes. But my sister doesn't it.

CHAPTER 02

명사, 관사, 대명사

명사의 종류와 수량 표현

1 명사의 의미와 종류

사람, 사물, 장소, 개념 등을 일컫는 말로, 셀 수 있는 명사와 셀 수 없는 명사로 나뉜다.

셀 수 있는 명사	bike, banana, boy, cat, girl, city, flower, team...
셀 수 없는 명사	Tony, Seoul, Korea, hope, beauty, paper, coffee...

2 명사의 복수형

규칙형	대부분 → -s	lakes, dogs, houses
	-s, -sh, -ch, -x, -o → -es	buses, benches, boxes, potatoes *예외: pianos, photos, radios
	자음+y → -ies	babies, cities, parties
	–f(e) → -ves	knives, leaves, wolves *예외: roofs, safes
불규칙형	불규칙	man → men, woman → women, tooth → teeth, foot → feet, goose → geese, child → children, ox → oxen, mouse → mice
예외	단수와 복수가 동일한 경우	deer, fish, sheep
	항상 복수인 경우	jeans, pants, scissors, socks

'모음 + y'로 끝나는 명사
- '모음+y'로 끝나는 명사는 그대로 -s만 붙인다.

  toy → toys, day → days

항상 복수로 쓰이는 명사
- 항상 복수로 쓰이는 명사는 a pair of를 사용한다.

  a pair of jeans[socks, pants]

3 명사의 수량 표현

	많은		약간의	거의 없는
수	many	a lot of (= lots of = plenty of)	a few	few
양	much		a little	little

I have many good ideas.

He has a little bread.

She doesn't have much money.

Mia has few friends.

4 물질 명사의 수량 표현

물질 명사란 특별한 형태가 없는 셀 수 없는 명사를 말하며, 단위 명사를 사용하여 센다.

a piece of	cheese, bread, cake, pizza	a slice of	cheese, pizza, bread
a cup of	coffee, tea	a bottle of	ink, juice, milk
a glass of	water, milk, beer	a pound of	sugar, meat
a loaf of	bread	a bowl of	soup, rice
a bar of	soap, chocolate		

물질 명사
- 물질 명사는 셀 수 없기 때문에 two cups of coffees라고 하지 않고 two cups of coffee라고 한다.

VOCA safe 금고 | goose 거위 | ox 황소 | pants 바지 | scissors 가위

Let's Check It Out

>>> 정답 4쪽

My score is
/ 19점

A   단어의 성격이 나머지 둘과 다른 것을 고르시오. 각 1점

1 ① peace   ② sadness   ③ tower
2 ① England   ② clock   ③ Shanghai
3 ① Wi-Fi   ② smartphone   ③ pen
4 ① paper   ② love   ③ pencil
5 ① dish   ② science   ③ key

B   명사의 복수형이 잘못된 것을 찾아 바르게 고치시오. 각 1점

1 ① eggs   ② beachs   ③ potatoes   → _____
2 ① radios   ② tomatos   ③ babies   → _____
3 ① fish   ② leaves   ③ geeses   → _____
4 ① toyes   ② tests   ③ problems   → _____

C   [   ]에서 알맞은 것을 고르시오. 각 1점

1 I have [many / much] coins.
2 You drink too [many / much] coke.
3 He needs [a lot of / many] attention.
4 I have [a few / a little] true friends.
5 There is [few / little] juice in the bottle.

D   [보기]에서 적절한 단어를 골라 빈칸에 알맞은 형태로 쓰시오. 각 1점

보기	pair	slice	bar	bowl	cup

1 He drinks five _____ of coffee every day.
2 That is a really big _____ of pizza.
3 I eat a _____ of soup for breakfast.
4 Do you have a _____ of scissors?
5 I have a _____ of chocolate in my bag.

VOCA   peace 평화 | sadness 슬픔 | coin 동전 | attention 관심, 주의

1 다음 중 단수-복수 형태가 잘못된 것은? 2점

① class – classes   ② wife – wives   ③ sheep – sheep
④ man – men   ⑤ key – keies

2 밑줄 친 부분의 쓰임이 어법상 어색한 것은? 2점

① I want a cup of coffee.
② She needs two pieces of paper.
③ I need a piece of pants.
④ I drink a bottle of water every day.
⑤ Put three glasses of milk into it.

3 How many sentences are grammatically wrong? 4점

ⓐ I have two sisters.
ⓑ Yeji has lots of friends.
ⓒ Two mice have two piece of cheeses.
ⓓ The lady has a large house in the city.
ⓔ The man has just a few bills.
ⓕ How many bread do you want?

① one   ② two   ③ three
④ four   ⑤ five

4 우리말과 일치하도록 빈칸에 알맞은 말을 쓰시오. 4점

외로운 효진은 친구가 거의 없다.

→ Lonely Hyojin has _____ _____.

5 Find TWO errors and correct them. 4점

인간은 두 손과 두 발이 있다.
= A human has two handes and two feets.

_____ → _____

_____ → _____

VOCA   bill 지폐 | lonely 외로운 | human 인간

30

06 부정관사와 정관사

부정관사 a/an

셀 수 있는 단수 명사 앞에 쓰며, 막연한 하나를 의미한다.

a+자음	a toy, a cat, a hospital
an+모음	an apple, an actor, an orange

Spiderman is a hero.

Takaki is a Japanese teacher.

She's an honest person.

Do you still have an MP3 player?

GRAMMAR POINT

모음

- 발음이 [a, e, i, o, u]인 음을 말하며 나머지는 자음이다.
- 부정관사의 쓰임은 철자가 아니라 발음으로 구분한다.

  a university, a uniform, an hour, an FBI agent

정관사 the

특정한 것을 나타내며, 다음과 같은 경우에 사용된다.

앞에 나온 명사를 다시 말할 때	I have a hamster. The hamster is very cute.
서로 알고 있는 것을 말할 때	Please open the window.
유일한 것을 나타낼 때	The Earth goes around the sun.
악기 이름 앞에	She often plays the guitar.
수식어구의 꾸밈을 받을 때	The gift on the table is from Hara.

관용적으로 the를 쓰는 경우

- in the morning
- in the afternoon
- in the evening
- on the Internet

관사를 쓰지 않는 경우

식사, 운동, 학과목 앞	breakfast, lunch, dinner, baseball, math
나라 이름, 도시 이름, 사람 이름 앞	Japan, Shanghai, Jason
by+교통수단	by bus, by taxi, by subway
소유격과 함께 쓰인 명사 앞	my sister, her bag, our room
장소나 건물이 본래의 목적으로 사용될 때	go to school, go to church

Lucy doesn't have breakfast.

Do you play golf?

Does she come from England?

I sometimes go to school by taxi.

on foot

- '걸어서'는 by foot이 아니라 on foot으로 쓴다.

식사명에 관사를 쓰는 경우

- 식사명에 형용사를 같이 쓰면 관사를 쓴다.

  a small breakfast

VOCA honest 정직한 | still 아직도 | hamster 햄스터 | often 종종 | sometimes 때때로 | university 대학 | agent 요원

Let's Check It Out

>>> 정답 4쪽

A 빈칸에 'a' 또는 'an'을 쓰고 필요가 없으면 ×표 하시오. 각 1점

1 ① _____ man   ② _____ milk   ③ _____ item

2 ① _____ dancer   ② _____ books   ③ _____ honest man

3 ① _____ hour   ② _____ soccer   ③ _____ soccer ball

4 ① _____ oil   ② _____ person   ③ _____ feet

5 ① _____ uniform   ② _____ salt   ③ _____ MVP

B [ ]에서 알맞은 것을 고르시오. 각 1점

1 She has a dog. [A / The] dog is very old.

2 Do you play [a / the] harp?

3 Will you close [a / the] door?

4 [The / A] moon is blue tonight.

5 [A / The] coffee in the cup is very hot.

C [보기]에서 빈칸에 알맞은 말을 골라 쓰시오. 각 1점

보기	a	an	the	× (관사 없음)

1 My favorite sport is _____ basketball.

2 Do you have _____ dinner at home?

3 Traveling by _____ subway is fast and comfortable.

4 Look at _____ beautiful rainbow over there.

5 Maria wants to be _____ engineer.

D 빈칸에 적절한 관사를 쓰고, 관사가 필요 없으면 ×표 하시오. 각 1점

1 Can you play _____ drum?

2 Dan plays _____ baseball with his father.

3 My aunt is _____ astronaut.

4 The students don't like _____ science.

5 She has _____ villa in Italy.

VOCA **item** 물건 | **MVP** 최우수 선수(most valuable player) | **harp** 하프 | **favorite** 제일 좋아하는 | **travel** 이동하다 | **comfortable** 편안한 | **engineer** 엔지니어, 기술자 | **astronaut** 우주 비행사 | **villa** 고급 주택, 별장

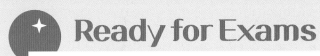

My score is

Let's Check It Out _____ / 20점   0~24점 → Level 1 Test
Ready for Exams _____ / 15점   25~29점 → Level 2 Test
Total _____ / 35점   30~35점 → Level 3 Test

Ready for Exams

>>> 정답 4쪽

1 Which blank does NOT need the word "a"? 2점

  ① My sister is _____ good student.

  ② This is _____ new chair.

  ③ I need _____ water, please.

  ④ He is _____ great inventor.

  ⑤ She doesn't have _____ laptop.

2 다음 대화의 빈칸에 들어갈 말로 알맞은 것은? 3점

> A: It's so hot in here. Turn on _____ air conditioner, please.
> B: Okay. I will.

  ① a   ② an   ③ the

  ④ its   ⑤ those

3 다음 중 어법상 어색한 문장을 모두 고르시오. 4점

  ① Everybody needs love.

  ② She plays soccer after school.

  ③ Her real name is the Bongsuk.

  ④ My a father is a businessman.

  ⑤ Mom, I want an one-dollar bill.

4 다음 동수와 Ronald의 등교 방법을 보고, 빈칸에 각각 두 단어를 써서 문장을 완성하시오.
각 3점

동수	walk
Ronald	bus

(1) Dongsu goes to school _____ _____.

(2) Ronald goes to school _____ _____.

VOCA inventor 발명가 | laptop 노트북 컴퓨터 | air conditioner 에어컨 | businessman 사업가

지시 · 재귀대명사, 비인칭 주어

CONCEPT 1 지시대명사

가까이 있는 것은 this와 these, 멀리 있는 것은 that과 those로 나타낸다.

단수	this	that
복수	these	those

This is my bat, and that's yours.

These are my oranges, but those are not mine.

CONCEPT 2 재귀대명사

인칭대명사에 –self/–selves를 더해 '자신(들)'이란 의미로 사용된다.

	단수	재귀대명사	복수	재귀대명사
1인칭	I	myself	we	ourselves
2인칭	you	yourself	you	yourselves
3인칭	he/she/it	himself/herself/itself	they	themselves

A 강조적 용법: 생략 가능

I do my homework myself. (주어 강조)

She likes her room itself. (목적어 강조)

B 재귀적 용법: 생략 불가능

Narcissus likes himself.

She often speaks to herself.

CONCEPT 3 비인칭 주어

it을 사용하여 아래와 같은 경우에 나타내며 해석은 하지 않는다.

날씨	It rains a lot in summer.
시간	What time is it? – It is 7:10.
날짜	It is February 28 today.
요일	Hooray! It's Sunday.
계절	Brrr... It's winter now.
명암	Look! It is bright outside.
거리	It's about 5km from Seoul.

GRAMMAR POINT

지시대명사를 받을 때

- this/that은 it으로, these/those는 they로 받는다.

  A: Is this yours?

  B: Yes, it is.

  A: Are those your pencils?

  B: No, they aren't.

지시형용사

- this/that/these/those는 명사 앞에서 지시형용사로도 사용된다.

  This knife is very sharp.

재귀대명사의 재귀적 용법

- 재귀대명사가 동사나 전치사 뒤에 오면 주로 재귀적 용법이다.

재귀대명사의 관용 표현

- by oneself: 홀로, 혼자
- for oneself: 스스로
- by[of] itself: 저절로

  He lives by himself.

  (그는 혼자 산다.)

  She fixes her computer for herself.

  (그녀는 스스로 컴퓨터를 고친다.)

  The door opens by[of] itself.

  (그 문은 저절로 열린다.)

it의 해석

- 비인칭 주어가 아닌 인칭대명사 it은 '그것'으로 해석한다.

  I'm sorry. It is my fault.

  (미안해. 그건 내 잘못이야.)

VOCA Narcissus 나르키소스(그리스 신화에 나오는 미소년) | speak to oneself 혼잣말하다 | hooray 만세 | brrr 부르르 | bright 밝은 | about 약 | sharp 날카로운 | fix 고치다 | fault 잘못

Let's Check It Out

››› 정답 4쪽

A [ ]에서 알맞은 것을 고르시오. 각 1점

1 [This / These] is my first time in Sejong.

2 Are [that / those] your classmates?

3 [This / These] are not yours.

4 Is this his? – No, [this / it] isn't.

5 Are those your dogs? – Yes, [they / those] are.

B 우리말과 같은 뜻이 되도록 밑줄 친 말을 바르게 고치시오. 각 1점

1 She loves her too much. (그녀는 스스로를 너무 사랑한다.) ➡ _____

2 They them are teachers. (그들 자신이 교사이다.) ➡ _____

3 Let me introduce me. (제 소개를 하겠습니다.) ➡ _____

4 The weather it is a problem. (날씨 자체가 문제이다.) ➡ _____

5 She goes to school for herself. (그녀는 혼자 등교한다.) ➡ _____

C 밑줄 친 단어의 쓰임이 [보기]와 같으면 =로, 아니면 ≠로 표시하시오. 각 1점

> 보기   She often looks at herself in the mirror.

1 I will do it myself. ➡ _____

2 The man paints himself. ➡ _____

3 Help yourself to the oranges. ➡ _____

4 Kimberly believes herself. ➡ _____

5 Mr. Kim himself cooks. ➡ _____

D 밑줄 친 'It[it]'이 '비인칭 주어'인지, '인칭대명사'인지 구분하시오. 각 1점

1 It is so fast. ➡ _____

2 What day is it? ➡ _____

3 Isn't it expensive? ➡ _____

4 It is 7 kilometers to school. ➡ _____

5 It is so hot here in Thailand. ➡ _____

VOCA   classmate 같은 반 친구 | too 너무 | introduce 소개하다 | mirror 거울 | paint 그리다 | help oneself 음식을 먹다 | believe 믿다 | Thailand 태국

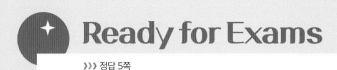

My score is

Let's Check It Out _____ / 20점	0~24점 → Level 1 Test
Ready for Exams _____ / 15점	25~29점 → Level 2 Test
Total _____ / 35점	30~35점 → Level 3 Test

Ready for Exams

>>> 정답 5쪽

1 Which is correct for the blank? 2점

> A: Are those your earrings?
> B: _____. I don't have any earrings.

① Yes, those are   ② Yes, they are   ③ No, those are

④ No, these aren't   ⑤ No, they aren't

2 밑줄 친 부분의 쓰임이 나머지와 <u>다른</u> 하나는? 2점

① Mom often speaks to <u>herself</u>.
② We enjoy <u>ourselves</u> at the pool.
③ Eva likes <u>herself</u> in a dress.
④ Sadly, Eddie hates <u>himself</u> a lot.
⑤ They <u>themselves</u> shoot the video.

3 다음 중 밑줄 친 'It[it]'의 쓰임이 [보기]와 <u>다른</u> 것을 <u>모두</u> 고르시오. 3점

> 보기   <u>It</u> is a sunny autumn day.

① <u>It</u> is five o'clock.   ② <u>It</u> is Monday today.   ③ Is <u>it</u> dark out there?

④ <u>It</u> is not my cat.   ⑤ <u>It</u> smells so good.

4 우리말을 영작한 문장에서 어법상 <u>어색한</u> 것을 찾아 바르게 고치시오. 4점

> 그는 거울로 자신을 보지 않는다.
> = He doesn't look at him in the mirror.

_____ ➡ _____

5 Look at the picture and complete the dialog. 4점

> A: _____ _____ Tuesday
>   today?
> B: No, _____ _____
>   Thursday.

CHAPTER 02
Review Test
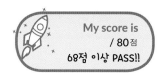
My score is
/ 80점
68점 이상 PASS!!

>>> 정답 5쪽

01 U05_2
다음 중 단수-복수 형태가 잘못된 것은? 2점

① a door – two doors
② a foot – three foots
③ a tomato – four tomatoes
④ a man – five men
⑤ a friend – six friends

02 U05_3

Find ALL possible answers for the blank. 2점

There are _____ students on the bus.

① little   ② a little
③ lots of   ④ much
⑤ a few

03 U05_4+GP

다음 중 밑줄 친 표현이 어색한 것은? 2점

① She has a pair of gloves.
② I want two loaves of bread.
③ Give him two sheets of paper.
④ Mom needs two piece of cheese now.
⑤ She drinks three glasses of milk every day.

04 U05_1+2+3
★
고난도
다음 중 어법상 옳은 것으로 묶인 것은? 3점

ⓐ We get a lot of snow in January.
ⓑ He has six best friend.
ⓒ I have a little questions.
ⓓ They are very kind teachers.
ⓔ There are sixty seconds in a minute.

① ⓐ   ② ⓐ, ⓑ, ⓓ
③ ⓐ, ⓓ, ⓔ   ④ ⓑ, ⓓ, ⓔ
⑤ ⓐ, ⓑ, ⓓ, ⓔ

05 U06_1+GP
빈칸에 들어갈 말이 다른 하나는? 2점

① We need _____ help.
② It's _____ American eagle.
③ This building has _____ elevator.
④ Do you have _____ umbrella?
⑤ He is _____ honest boy.

06 U07_2

밑줄 친 부분을 생략할 수 없는 것끼리 묶인 것은? 2점

ⓐ She enjoys herself in the yard.
ⓑ I sometimes make pizza for myself.
ⓒ Mr. Miller himself likes beer.
ⓓ The car door locks by itself.
ⓔ I will introduce myself to you.
ⓕ The vacuum cleaner itself cleans the house.

① ⓒ, ⓔ   ② ⓐ, ⓑ, ⓓ
③ ⓑ, ⓓ, ⓔ   ④ ⓐ, ⓑ, ⓓ, ⓔ
⑤ ⓐ, ⓒ, ⓓ, ⓔ

07 U06_3
Which translation is right? 2점

그는 아침을 먹고 학교로 뛰어간다.

① He runs to school after the breakfast.
② He runs to school after a breakfast.
③ He runs to school after breakfast.
④ After a breakfast, he runs to school.
⑤ After the breakfast, he runs to school.

08 U06_1+GP
빈칸에 들어갈 표현을 바르게 쓰지 못한 학생은? 2점

My new neighbor is a _____.

① 정하: great liar
② 현진: old but strong man
③ 희숙: smartphone seller
④ 가람: British pilot
⑤ 별이: cool guitarist in a band

09 다음 빈칸에 알맞지 <u>않은</u> 것은? 2점

함정

> Christine has _____, but she wants to buy more.

① two pairs of sneakers
② plenty of blouse
③ a lot of baseball caps
④ many scarves
⑤ some cute swimsuits

10 밑줄 친 'It[it]'의 쓰임이 나머지와 <u>다른</u> 것은? 2점

한눈에 쏙

① <u>It</u> is eight forty-five.
② <u>It</u> is so warm this morning.
③ Is <u>it</u> Friday today?
④ <u>It</u> is too dark in here.
⑤ <u>It</u> is a very cold country.

11 주어진 단어들을 조합하여 어법상 옳은 문장을 만들 수 <u>없는</u> 것은? 4점

★ 고난도

① is / a / . / My / watch / phone / just
② soap / . / bars / bought / two / I / of
③ parents / She / honor / a / to / . / is / her
④ are / firefighers / . / women / not / These
⑤ in / . / has / his / a / safes / few / basement / He

12 우리말을 영작할 때 빈칸에 들어갈 수 <u>없는</u> 것은? (정답 2개) 2점

> 좋은 나무가 좋은 과일을 만든다.
> = A _____ tree _____ _____
> _____ .

① good   ② is
③ makes   ④ produce
⑤ fruit

13 밑줄 친 부분 중 어법상 <u>어색한</u> 것은? (정답 최대 3개) 3점

★ 고난도

① He has <u>little</u> secrets.
② She drinks <u>a little</u> water.
③ I don't have <u>many</u> change.
④ There are <u>few</u> visitors today.
⑤ Aria spends <u>lots of</u> money with me.

14 다음 우리말을 영어로 바르게 옮긴 것은? 2점

> 우리 호텔에는 많은 재능 있는 요리사들이 있습니다.

① We has many talented chefs at our hotel.
② We have much talented chefs at our hotel.
③ We have plenty of talented chefs at our hotel.
④ We have lots of talented chef at our hotel.
⑤ We have many talented chefes at our hotel.

15 다음 문장에서 <u>어색한</u> 것을 찾아 바르게 고친 것은? 2점

> His cousins doesn't live in an one-room apartment.

① His → Him
② cousins → cousines
③ doesn't → aren't
④ live → lives
⑤ an → a

16 밑줄 친 부분의 쓰임이 [보기]와 같은 것은? 2점

> Monica doesn't do the dishes <u>herself</u>.

① Nicole doesn't love <u>herself</u>.
② Luka teaches his daughter <u>herself</u>.
③ Kelly goes to school by <u>herself</u>.
④ Juhee controls <u>herself</u> very well.
⑤ Hijin often takes pictures of <u>herself</u>.

17 U05_3
다음 빈칸에 알맞은 것을 <u>모두</u> 고르시오. 4점

There are a few _____ in the water.

ⓐ fish   ⓑ child   ⓒ swimmers
ⓓ divers   ⓔ girls   ⓕ duck
ⓖ boats   ⓗ flower

→ _____

18 U05_2+07_1
[보기]와 같이 괄호 안의 단어를 사용해서 주어진 문장을 바꿔 쓰시오. 4점

보기 A boy plays with a duck. (boys)
      → Boys play with ducks.

Is that your baby? (those)

→ _____

19 U05_4
우리말과 같은 뜻이 되도록 빈칸을 채우시오. 4점
함정

그는 겨울에 양말 두 켤레를 신는다.

→ He wears _____ in
winter.

20 U05_3
다음을 조건에 맞도록 영작할 때 앞에서부터 <u>3번째로</u> 올 단어를 쓰시오. 4점

그녀는 주머니에 돈이 거의 없다.

· 조건 1 She를 가장 먼저 쓸 것
· 조건 2 doesn't를 쓰지 말 것

→ _____

21 U05_2+U06_2
Look at the picture and complete the sentence. Use the given word. 4점

→ Two _____ are on _____
lake. (goose)

22 U06_3
다음 중 어법상 <u>어색한</u> 것을 찾아 바르게 고치시오. 4점

ⓐ Kate plays the drum very well.
ⓑ She has a dinner with her family.
ⓒ We are from New York, New York.

( ) _____ → _____

23 U07_2
주어진 단어 중 <u>필요한</u> 것만 골라 영작하시오. 4점

강 씨는 자신을 그들에게 소개한다.
him, them, himself, themselves, to

→ Mr. Kang introduces _____ .

24 U06_2+3
Find ALL of the errors and correct them. 5점

I go to school in Ilsan. A school is not far from
my house. But I usually go there by the taxi.

→ _____

25 U06_1+3+GP
다음 중 어법상 <u>어색한</u> 문장의 첫 글자를 차례대로 써서 주어진 문장을 완성하시오. 6점
★ 고난도

ⓐ He goes to school on foot.
ⓑ My little brother wears an uniform.
ⓒ There is a MP3 file in the folder.
ⓓ I skip a breakfast every morning.
ⓔ New Castle is my teacher's hometown.
ⓕ Peter and Ted play the ping-pong together.
ⓖ He has an old car.

→ ☐y ☐eacher ☐s ☐retty.

26 U06_1+2+GP
Find ALL of the errors in the underlined words and correct them. 5점
함정

Mrs. Choi has ⓐthree children: a boy and
ⓑtwo girls. ⓒA boy is ⓓa elementary
school student, and ⓔgirls are ⓕa university
students.

→ _____

_____

한눈에 쏙! 아래 노트를 보면서 빈칸을 채워 보세요.

1 명사의 수량 표현

수	many	a lot of[2)_____ of,	4)_____, a 4)_____
양	1)_____	3)_____] of	little, a little
물질명사	a 5)p_____ of cake, two 6)p_____ of meat, three 7)l_____ of bread		

2 부정관사

(a+자음)   (1)_____+모음)

⟶ ⊛발음이 모음일 때

3 재귀대명사

(1)_____ 용법)   (재귀적 용법)   (관용 표현)

⟶ 생략 가능   ⟶ 생략 2)_____   ⟶ 생략 3)_____

4 비인칭 주어

(날씨) (1)시_) (날짜) (2)요_) (계절) (3)명_) (4)거_)

cf. 인칭대명사 5)_____ (그것)

헷갈리지 말자! 초록색으로 표시된 부분을 바르게 고쳐 쓰세요.

1 They have <u>few gooses</u> but <u>many deers</u>.

⟶   ⟶

2 ⓐ They hate the work <u>itself</u>.

ⓑ He looks at <u>himself</u> in the window.

➡ ⓐ는 재귀적 용법, ⓑ는 강조적 용법이며 ⓐ는 생략 가능하다.

⟶   ⟶

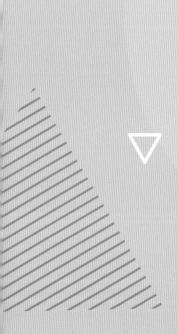

CHAPTER 03
시제

1 be동사의 과거형

am과 is의 과거형은 was이고 are의 과거형은 were이며 '~이었다, (~에) 있었다'라고 해석한다.

주어	현재	과거
I	am	was
He/She/It	is	
You/We/They	are	were

My grandfather was in the garden.

She was excited about the trip.

You were so cute.

The teachers were very angry.

2 be동사 과거형의 부정문

be동사 과거형의 부정문은 was/were not이며 '~이 아니었다, (~에) 있지 않았다'라고 해석한다.

주어	현재	과거
I	am not	was not[wasn't]
He/She/It	is not[isn't]	
You/We/They	are not[aren't]	were not[weren't]

I was not at school.

Billy was not my student.

They weren't satisfied.

3 be동사 과거형의 의문문과 대답

「Was/Were + 주어 ~?」의 형태로 묻고, be동사의 과거형을 써서 대답한다.

의문문	대답	
Was/Were + 주어 ~?	긍정	Yes, 주어 + was/were.
	부정	No, 주어 + wasn't/weren't.

I was stupid. → Was I stupid? – Yes, you were. / No, you weren't.

It was his fault. → Was it his fault? – Yes, it was. / No, it wasn't.

They were good friends.→ Were they good friends?

– Yes, they were. / No, they weren't.

GRAMMAR POINT

과거를 나타내는 부사(구)

• last night, yesterday, a few days ago와 같이 과거를 나타내는 부사(구)가 있으면 과거를 쓴다.

• They are (→ were) at the subway station last night.

VOCA garden 정원, 텃밭 | excited 흥분한, 신이 난 | satisfied 만족한 | fault 잘못

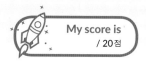

Let's Check It Out

》》》 정답 6쪽

A [ ]에서 알맞은 것을 고르시오. 각 1점

1 I [was / were] very tired yesterday.

2 She [was / were] in her room all day.

3 Chris [was / were] sad.

4 They [was / were] at the office.

5 The boy [is / was] 13 years old last year.

B 빈칸에 be동사 과거형의 부정형을 줄임말로 쓰시오. 각 1점

1 She _____ at home.

2 We _____ very happy.

3 Sorry. It _____ you.

4 You _____ born at that time.

5 Your tooth _____ good.

C 다음을 의문문으로 바꿀 때 빈칸에 알맞은 말을 쓰시오. 각 1점

1 They were busy.

→ _____ they busy?

2 It was rainy yesterday.

→ _____ _____ rainy yesterday?

3 The mirror was broken.

→ _____ _____ _____ broken?

4 Your mother was a cheerleader.

→ _____ _____ _____ a cheerleader?

5 She and you were at the plaza.

→ _____ _____ _____ _____ at the plaza?

D 밑줄 친 부분을 바르게 고치시오. 각 1점

1 The babies <u>was</u> very sleepy. → _____

2 The pencils <u>not were</u> very good. → _____

3 Ethics <u>weren't</u> my favorite class. → _____

4 <u>Was</u> the tickets sold out? → _____

5 I <u>am</u> in the same class as Miki last year. → _____

VOCA at that time 그때에, 당시에 | broken 깨진 | cheerleader 치어리더 | plaza 광장 | ethics 윤리 | sold out 매진된

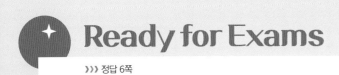

Ready for Exams

>>> 정답 6쪽

My score is

Let's Check It Out _____ / 20점   0~24점 → Level 1 Test
Ready for Exams _____ / 15점   25~29점 → Level 2 Test
Total _____ / 35점   30~35점 → Level 3 Test

1 빈칸에 들어갈 말이 나머지와 <u>다른</u> 하나는? 2점

① We _____ in the Sahara Desert at that time.

② Carl and I _____ busy last weekend.

③ She _____ very popular at the party yesterday.

④ Your kids _____ late again this morning.

⑤ They _____ in Manchester last year.

2 다음 중 밑줄 친 부분이 어법상 <u>어색한</u> 것은? 2점

① She <u>wasn't</u> in the bathroom.

② I <u>was not</u> at the snack bar.

③ Harris <u>not</u> was here yesterday.

④ Rocky and Rex <u>weren't</u> ready at all.

⑤ They <u>were not</u> at the restaurant last night.

3 Which is correct for the blank? 2점

_____ you at the party last night?

① Are   ② Was   ③ Were

④ Is   ⑤ Am

4 다음 중 어법상 <u>어색한</u> 것을 <u>2개</u> 찾아 바르게 고치시오. 4점

ⓐ I am 13 years old last year.

ⓑ She and I were on the same bus this morning.

ⓒ Were your new teacher kind to you?

(   ) _____ ➡ _____

(   ) _____ ➡ _____

5 주어진 단어 중 <u>필요한</u> 것만 골라 문장을 완성하시오. 5점

am, in the backseat, was, Gary, and I, are, were

➡ _____ that night.

VOCA   **Sahara Desert** 사하라 사막 | **popular** 인기 있는 | **Manchester** 맨체스터(영국 랭커셔주의 상공업 도시) | **ready** 준비된 | **not ~ at all**
전혀 ~ 아닌 | **backseat** 뒷좌석

UNIT 09 일반동사의 과거형

CONCEPT 1 일반동사의 과거형

A 규칙 동사: 일반동사의 원형에 -d나 -ed를 붙인다.

대부분의 동사	+-ed	called, worked, passed
-e로 끝나는 동사	+-d	danced, moved, saved
'자음+y'로 끝나는 동사	y → i+-ed	studied, worried, cried
'단모음+단자음'으로 끝나는 동사	자음+자음+-ed	shopped, stopped, planned

B 불규칙 동사: 과거형이 불규칙하게 변한다.

come – came	go – went	do – did	have – had
say – said	drink – drank	meet – met	teach – taught
get – got	speak – spoke	think – thought	find – found
buy – bought	bring – brought	take – took	sit – sat
hit – hit	cut – cut	hurt – hurt	read [ri:d] – read [red]

CONCEPT 2 일반동사 과거형의 부정문

일반동사 과거형의 부정문은 「did not[didn't] +동사원형」의 형태로 쓴다.

> did not[didn't] +동사원형

Your dad lived here. → Your dad did not live here.

She did her best. → She didn't do her best.

CONCEPT 3 일반동사 과거형의 의문문

「Did+주어+동사원형 ~?」의 형태로 묻고, did를 사용하여 대답한다.

의문문		대답
Did+주어+동사원형 ~?	긍정	Yes, 주어+did.
	부정	No, 주어+did not[didn't].

Your son swam in the pool. → Did your son swim in the pool?

– Yes, he did. / No, he didn't.

They came home early. → Did they come home early?

– Yes, they did. / No, they didn't.

GRAMMAR POINT

'모음+y'로 끝나는 동사

• '모음+y'로 끝나는 동사에는 -ed 만 붙인다.

We really <u>enjoyed</u> your show, Mr. Bernard.

불규칙 동사의 과거형

• 불규칙 동사의 과거형은 p. 149의 불규칙 동사 변화표 참조.

조동사 did

• did ~가 나오면 본동사는 원형으로 써야 한다.

She did not ~~said~~ (→ say) a word.

Did he ~~caught~~ (→ catch) a lot of fish?

VOCA do one's best 최선을 다하다

Let's Check It Out

>>> 정답 6쪽

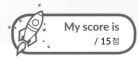

My score is
/ 15점

A 동사의 과거형을 쓰시오. 각 1점

1 ① do   → _____   ② have   → _____

2 ① hit   → _____   ② go   → _____

3 ① run   → _____   ② try   → _____

4 ① see   → _____   ② catch   → _____

B 빈칸에 알맞은 동사를 [보기]에서 골라 과거형으로 쓰시오. 각 1점

| 보기 | read | put | sell | make | visit |

1 She _____ handmade soap.

2 We _____ Alcatraz.

3 I _____ the news in the morning.

4 Gabbie _____ a paper swan.

5 The boy _____ on his swimming cap.

C 다음을 부정문으로 바꿀 때 빈칸에 알맞은 말을 쓰시오. 각 1점

1 She skipped breakfast today.

  → She _____ _____ breakfast today.

2 My grandmother wore glasses.

  → My grandmother _____ _____ glasses.

3 I did my homework before dinner.

  → I _____ _____ my homework before dinner.

D 다음을 의문문으로 바꿀 때 빈칸에 알맞은 말을 쓰시오. 각 1점

1 You drove my car.

  → _____ _____ _____ my car?

2 They liked the design of the floor.

  → _____ _____ _____ the design of the floor?

3 He paid ten dollars for the app.

  → _____ _____ _____ ten dollars for the app?

VOCA handmade 수제의, 손으로 만든 | Alcatraz 앨커트래즈(예전에 교도소가 있었던, 샌프란시스코 연안의 작은 섬) | paper swan 종이학 | put on 쓰다, 입다 |
swimming cap 수영 모자 | skip 거르다 | design 디자인 | pay 지불하다 | app 앱, 어플

46

My score is

Let's Check It Out _____ / 15점   0~17점 → Level 1 Test
Ready for Exams _____ / 10점   ➡   18~21점 → Level 2 Test
Total _____ / 25점   22~25점 → Level 3 Test

Ready for Exams

>>> 정답 6쪽

1   다음 각 빈칸에 들어갈 말이 바르게 짝지어진 것은? 2점

> • He _____ his teeth three times every day.
> • He _____ his teeth three times yesterday.

① brush – brush   ② brushes – brushs   ③ brushes – brushed
④ brushs – brushed   ⑤ brushd – brushd

2   Which is NOT right for the blank? (2 answers) 2점

> He _____ last night.

① didn't found his wallet
② drinks a glass of milk
③ drove to the new mart
④ didn't have a big dinner
⑤ did not watch a horror movie

3   Find the sentence that has an error and correct it. 3점

> ⓐ Did you spent Valentine's Day alone?
> ⓑ Did she finally buy a smartphone?

(   ) _____ ➡ _____

4   그림을 보고 주어진 단어를 써서 문장을 완성하시오. 3점

➡ This morning, the soldier _____ a lizard and _____ it.
(catch, eat)

VOCA   brush one's teeth 이를 닦다 | horror movie 공포 영화 | soldier 군인 | lizard 도마뱀

UNIT 10 진행 시제

CONCEPT 1 -ing 만드는 법

대부분의 동사	+-ing	reading, jumping, eating
'자음+-e'로 끝나는 동사	-e를 빼고 +-ing	coming, closing, moving
-ie로 끝나는 경우	-ie → y+-ing	dying, lying, tying
'단모음＋단자음'으로 끝나는 동사	자음＋자음+-ing	running, putting, swimming, beginning

CONCEPT 2 현재 진행형

「am/is/are＋-ing」 형태로 '～하고 있다, ～하는 중이다'로 해석한다.

기본형	am/is/are＋-ing	
부정형	am not / is not[isn't] / are not[aren't]＋-ing	
의문문	Am/Is/Are＋주어＋-ing ～?	
	긍정의 대답	Yes, 주어＋am/is/are.
	부정의 대답	No, 주어＋am not / is not[isn't] / are not[aren't].

She is listening to my song.

She is not listening to my song.

Is she listening to my song? – Yes, she is. / No, she isn't.

CONCEPT 3 과거 진행형

「was/were＋-ing」 형태로 '～하고 있었다, ～하는 중이었다'로 해석한다.

기본형	was/were＋-ing	
부정형	was not[wasn't] / were not[weren't]＋-ing	
의문문	Was/Were＋주어＋-ing ～?	
	긍정의 대답	Yes, 주어＋was/were.
	부정의 대답	No, 주어＋was not[wasn't] / were not[weren't].

They were helping the old lady.

They weren't helping the old lady.

Were they helping the old lady? – Yes, they were. / No, they weren't.

GRAMMAR POINT

'자음＋y'로 끝나는 동사

• '자음＋y'로 끝나는 동사는 과거형과는 달리 -ing만 붙인다.

studying, crying, trying

진행형으로 쓰지 않는 동사

• 소유, 감정, 인식 등을 나타내는 동사는 진행형으로 쓰지 않는다.

have(가지다), like, love, become, know 등

She is having (→ has) two daughters.

Now I am understanding (→ understand) your plan.

• have가 '먹다', '시간을 보내다'의 뜻일 때는 진행형으로 쓸 수 있다.

Are you having fun?

He is having lunch over there.

VOCA understand 이해하다 | plan 계획

Let's Check It Out

>>> 정답 6쪽

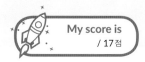

A 동사의 –ing형을 쓰시오. 각 1점

1 ① walk → _____ ② love → _____

2 ① play → _____ ② put → _____

3 ① lie → _____ ② see → _____

4 ① run → _____ ② watch → _____

5 ① climb → _____ ② shop → _____

B 괄호 안의 단어를 이용하여 현재 진행형 문장을 완성하시오. 각 1점

1 Her mother _____ _____ dinner now. (cook)

2 She _____ _____ push-ups. (do)

3 Tanya _____ _____ with George. (not, dance)

4 The kids _____ _____ at me. (laugh)

5 _____ you guys _____ fun? (have)

C 문장을 과거 진행형으로 바꿀 때 빈칸에 알맞은 말을 쓰시오. 각 1점

1 He planned a vacation.

  → He _____ _____ a vacation.

2 She carried a watermelon.

  → She _____ _____ a watermelon.

3 They didn't look at me.

  → They _____ _____ at me.

4 He didn't smile at us.

  → He _____ _____ at us.

D 문장을 괄호 안의 지시대로 바꾸어 쓰시오. 각 1점

1 Strangers visit my homepage. (진행형)

  → Strangers _____ my homepage.

2 The monkey didn't eat the banana. (진행형)

  → The monkey _____ the banana.

3 You were waiting for Grace. (의문문)

  → _____ for Grace?

VOCA **push-up** 팔 굽혀 펴기 | **have fun** 재미있게 놀다 | **carry** 옮기다, 나르다 | **stranger** 낯선 사람 | **visit** 방문하다

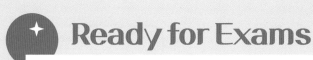
1   다음 중 동사의 –ing형이 잘못된 것의 개수는? 2점

dying	swiming	opening	dancing	becoming
cutting	sking	catchying	helpping	flying

① 2개   ② 3개   ③ 4개

④ 5개   ⑤ 6개

2   Who rewrites the sentence correctly? 3점

① 찬미: She studies Japanese. → She is studing Japanese.

② 미소: He lies on the grass. → He is lying on the grass.

③ 소현: I do not have a hard time. → I not having a hard time.

④ 현제: He doesn't play the cello. → He isn't plaing the cello.

⑤ 제민: She writes with her left hand. → She is writeing with her left hand.

3   다음 대화의 각 빈칸에 들어갈 말이 순서대로 나열된 것은? 3점

> A: _____ you feeding the dog?
> B: No, I _____. I _____ training him.

① Are – wasn't – was

② Are – was not – am

③ Were – weren't – were

④ Were – wasn't – am

⑤ Were – wasn't – was

4   괄호 안의 단어를 이용하여 대화의 빈칸에 알맞은 말을 쓰시오. 5점

> Ava: Baby, where are you? What _____ you _____?
>   (do)
> Liam: I'm upstairs. I _____ _____ FIFA online.
>   (play) Hmm, I _____ something good. (smell)
> Ava: I'm _____ some pasta. (cook)

VOCA   grass 잔디밭 | have a hard time 어려움을 겪다 | feed 먹이를 주다 | train 훈련시키다 | upstairs 위층에 | online 온라인으로 | smell
냄새를 맡다, ~한 냄새가 나다

CHAPTER 03
Review Test
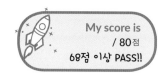

My score is
/ 80점
68점 이상 PASS!!

>>> 정답 7쪽

01 ^{U08_1} 다음 빈칸에 적절한 것을 <u>모두</u> 고르시오. 2점

> The world _____ mine.

① is   ② was
③ am   ④ were
⑤ are

02 ^{U08_1} 다음 빈칸에 알맞지 <u>않은</u> 것은? 2점

> Were _____ K-pop singers?

① you
② Mr. Jeong
③ they
④ your cousins
⑤ Shao and Celica

03 ^{U08_1+2+3} 다음 중 어법상 옳은 것은? 2점

① She wasn't my friend.
② Were your hourly pay good?
③ Was her sisters at the mall?
④ Her parents was nice to me.
⑤ He and I was in the chorus last year.

04 ^{U09_1B} Which is NOT proper for the blank? 2점

> The boy _____ a book at the bookstore.

① stole   ② got
③ bought   ④ found
⑤ readed

05 ^{U09_1B} 다음 중 어법상 옳은 것을 <u>모두</u> 고르시오. 3점

★고난도

① He cought a fish with his hand.
② She woke up early in the morning.
③ She braught a red flower to me.
④ His father bought a nice bike for him.
⑤ She thought about her father all day.

06 ^{U10_2} 다음 빈칸에 가장 적절한 것은? 2점

> I don't live here. But my aunt lives here. I am just _____ her.

① going   ② walking
③ visiting   ④ living
⑤ looking

07 ^{U09_3} 다음 대답이 나올 수 있는 질문으로 적절한 것은? 2점

> No, I didn't. I just gave it to my sister.

① Were you angry with her?
② Do you like animation movies?
③ Did you sell your backpack?
④ Did you give the cake to your sister?
⑤ Did you buy the blue dress?

08 ^{U10_2} Which dialog is <u>unnatural</u>? 2점

① A: Does Hayun live here?
   B: No, he doesn't.
② A: What are they doing?
   B: They sing and dance.
③ A: How old is your teacher?
   B: I don't know.
④ A: Try this. It's tasty.
   B: No, thanks. I'm not hungry.
⑤ A: What is she wearing?
   B: A pink shirt and blue jeans.

09 각 빈칸에 들어갈 말이 바르게 짝지어진 것은? 2점

- Sally is a shy girl. She _____ talk much.
- Mickey woke up late, so he _____ have breakfast.

① don't – doesn't
② doesn't – doesn't
③ doesn't – didn't
④ didn't – didn't
⑤ didn't – doesn't

10 어법상 올바르지 <u>않은</u> 것으로 묶인 것은? 3점

★ 고난도

ⓐ They were slept on the floor.
ⓑ Birds were flying in the sky.
ⓒ I'm sorry. I wasn't listening to you.
ⓓ The man was running fast now.
ⓔ She was having two sons and a daughter.

① ⓐ, ⓒ
② ⓐ, ⓓ
③ ⓒ, ⓔ
④ ⓐ, ⓒ, ⓔ
⑤ ⓐ, ⓓ, ⓔ

11 밑줄 친 부분 중 어법상 <u>어색한</u> 것은? (정답 최대 3개) 2점

 함정

① Jenny <u>was</u> poor at art.
② She <u>weren't</u> angry at him.
③ My sister <u>wasn't</u> a fast learner.
④ Colin and I <u>wasn't</u> very close.
⑤ <u>Was</u> they in the same office?

12 밑줄 친 부분 중 어법상 <u>어색한</u> 것을 바르게 고친 것은?
(정답 2개) 2점

This morning, I <u>finded</u> a coin on <u>the</u> floor. <u>It</u> <u>was</u> <u>her</u>.

① finded → found
② the → a
③ it → they
④ was → is
⑤ her → hers

13 다음 대화의 빈칸에 들어갈 말로 가장 적절한 것은? 2점

A: _____?
B: No, they didn't. They lost.

① Are Alice and Ryan lost
② Did they win the game
③ Were they playing the game
④ Are Gina and Mina at the stadium
⑤ Did Rocky and Zinna lose the game

14 다음 빈칸에 들어갈 말로 적절하지 <u>않은</u> 것은? 2점

She cut the meat into cubes _____.

① yesterday
② tomorrow
③ last night
④ two days ago
⑤ a few weeks ago

15 주어진 단어들을 조합하여 어법상 옳은 문장을 만들 수 없는 것은? 4점

★ 고난도

① a / ball / he / the wall. / threw / to
② had / beautiful / garden. / a / they
③ eyes / I / and / my / covered / cried.
④ did / English / at / taught / she / school?
⑤ car. / dad / an / expensive / my / bought

16 문장을 진행형으로 바르게 고치지 <u>못한</u> 것은? 2점

 한눈에 쏙

① I don't do that.
→ I am not doing that.
② He talks on the phone.
→ He is talking on the phone.
③ Do you listen to me?
→ Are you listening to me?
④ She doesn't have broccoli.
→ She isn't having broccoli.
⑤ The dog sat on the couch.
→ The dog was siting on the couch.

U08_2

17 Change the sentence like the example. 4점

> 보기 Brenda is happy now. (last night)
> → Brenda was not happy last night.
>
> The singer is famous now. (a few years ago)

→ _____

U08_2

18 다음을 조건에 맞게 영작하시오. 5점

> 난 어제 집에 있지 않았다.
>
> ·조건 1 be동사를 사용할 것
> ·조건 2 어휘 – at home
> ·조건 3 6단어로 쓸 것

→ _____

U08_3

19 다음 대화에서 어법상 어색한 것을 찾아 고치시오. 4점

> A: Are you Leo's classmates last year?
> B: No, we weren't.

_____ → _____

U08_1

20 빈칸에 들어갈 말이 같은 문장들의 첫 글자를 써서 주어진 문장을 완성하시오. 4점

한눈에 쏙

> ⓐ Cathy's books _____ not on the desk this morning.
> ⓑ Their store _____ very large before.
> ⓒ Ryan and his brother _____ short a few years ago.
> ⓓ Elephants _____ happy in the past.
> ⓔ Those people _____ not faithful then.

→ Your answer is ☐O☐R☐C☐.

U09_1B

21 Find the error and correct it. 4점

> Moon Ikjeom brings cotton seeds in the 15th century.
>
> *cotton seed: 목화씨

_____ → _____

U08_2+U09_2

22 다음 두 문장을 부정문으로 바꿔 쓰시오. 각 3점

(1) They were the same price.

→ _____

(2) My niece ran a marathon.

→ _____

U09_3

23 Write the common word for the blanks. 4점

> A: _____ you have a good time yesterday?
> B: Yes, I _____.

→ _____

U08_1+U09_1A+1B+U10+1+3

24 밑줄 친 부분 중 어법상 어색한 것을 3개 골라 바르게 고치시오. 각 3점

★ 고난도

> Yesterday, it ⓐwas a lovely morning, so we all ⓑwent to the pool. We ⓒsaw Mr. Porter and Dave there. They ⓓwere swiming. The sun ⓔwas shining, but later it ⓕwas becoming cloudy, so we ⓖhurryed home.

( ) → _____
( ) → _____
( ) → _____

U10_1+2+3

25 [보기]처럼 주어진 단어를 이용하여 문장을 2개 쓰시오. 각 2점

> 보기 (draw, the trees)
> → I am drawing the trees.
> → I was drawing the trees.
>
> (tie, my shoelaces)

→ _____

→ _____

한눈에 쏙! 아래 노트를 보면서 빈칸을 채워 보세요.

1 be동사의 과거형

과거형	부정문	의문문	대답
1) _____	2) _____ not = wasn't	Was+주어 ~?	Yes, 3) _____ +was. 4) _____, 주어+was not[wasn't].
were	were not = 5) _____	6) _____ +주어 ~?	Yes, 주어+7) _____ . No, 주어+8) _____ not[weren't].

2 일반동사의 과거형

동사	과거형	부정문	의문문	대답
move	1) _____			Yes, 5) _____ +did.
worry	2) _____	4) _____ +동사원형	Did+주어+동사원형 ~?	No, 6) _____ +did not [7) _____].
plan	3) _____			

3 진행 시제

	진행형	부정문	의문문	대답
현재	am/are/is+1) _____	be동사+3) _____	be동사+5) _____	Yes, 주어 +6) _____ .
과거	was/were+2) _____	+4) _____	+-ing ~?	No, 주어+be동사+not.

헷갈리지 말자! 초록색으로 표시된 부분을 바르게 고쳐 쓰세요.

1 I <u>am</u> so happy a few days ago.

2 Were Tammy and Jin nice to you? – No, <u>they were</u>.

3 Your daughter <u>did not came</u> to school today.

CHAPTER 04
조동사

UNIT 11 can, may

CONCEPT 1 조동사의 쓰임

조동사는 동사의 뜻을 보충해 주며, 주어의 인칭이나 수에 따라 변하지 않고 뒤에 반드시 동사원형이 온다.

평서문	주어＋조동사＋동사원형		
부정문	주어＋조동사＋not＋동사원형		
의문문	조동사＋주어＋동사원형 ～?	대답	Yes, 주어＋조동사. No, 주어＋조동사＋not.

CONCEPT 2 조동사 can (과거형: could)

뒤에 동사원형이 오며, 능력, 가능성, 허락의 뜻으로 나눌 수 있다.

	평서문	부정문	의문문	
형태	can＋동사원형	cannot[can't]＋동사원형	Can＋주어＋동사원형 ～?	
능력	～할 수 있다 (= be able to)	～할 수 없다 (= be not able to)	대답	Yes, 주어＋can. No, 주어＋can't.
가능성	～일 수도 있다	～일 리가 없다		
허락	～해도 된다 (= may)	～하면 안 된다 (= may not)		

She can (= is able to) speak Japanese. (능력)

Can (= May) I sit here? (허락) – Yes, you can. / No, you can't.

CONCEPT 3 조동사 may (과거형: might)

뒤에 동사원형이 오며, 약한 추측과 허락의 뜻으로 나눌 수 있다.

	평서문	부정문	의문문	
형태	may＋동사원형	may not＋동사원형	May＋주어＋동사원형 ～?	
약한 추측	～일지도 모른다	～이 아닐지도 모른다	대답	Yes, 주어＋may. No, 주어＋may not.
허락	～해도 된다 (= can)	～하면 안 된다 (= cannot)		

He may be rich. (추측)

You may go first. (허락)

You may not go first. (허락의 부정 – 금지)

GRAMMAR POINT

조동사의 중복

- 조동사 두 개는 나란히 쓸 수 없다.
  He ~~will can~~ win first prize. (×)
  → He will be able to win first prize. (○)

조동사 형태 불변

- 3인칭 단수 주어라도 조동사에는 -(e)s가 붙지 않는다.

be able to

- 조동사 can이 능력, 가능의 뜻일 때만 be able to로 비꾸어 쓸 수 있다. 허락의 뜻일 때는 may로 바꾸어 쓸 수 있으나 be able to로는 바꾸어 쓸 수 없다.

조동사 could의 두 가지 뜻

- can의 과거
  She could skate like a pro at the age of 7.
- 부탁 또는 요청하는 문장에서 공손함을 표현한다.
  Could you pass me the salt, please?

might의 두 가지 뜻

- may의 과거형
  He said he might come.
- 현재나 미래에 대해 may보다 더 불확실한 추측을 나타낼 때
  He might be rich.
  (그는 아마 부자일 것이다.)

VOCA　Japanese 일본어 | first prize 1등상 | pro 프로 선수

Let's Check It Out

»»» 정답 8쪽

A [   ]에서 알맞은 말을 고르시오. 각 1점

1 My father can [repairs / repair] my computer.
2 Debra [can / cans] dance well.
3 [Can you / Are you can] drive a car?
4 He [can't / doesn't can] ride a bike.
5 I [am / do] able to swim.

B 다음 문장을 'be able to'를 이용하여 바꿀 때 빈칸에 알맞은 말을 쓰시오. 각 1점

1 The little girl can jump rope well.
   → The little girl _____ _____ _____ jump rope well.
2 My dad can't play the guitar.
   → My dad _____ _____ _____ play the guitar.
3 Can you jump across the stream?
   → _____ _____ _____ _____ jump across the stream?

C 밑줄 친 조동사가 '추측'의 의미인지 '허락'의 의미인지 구분하시오. 각 1점

1 Can I take a break?   → _____
2 It may rain tomorrow.   → _____
3 May I ask you something?   → _____

D 우리말과 같은 뜻이 되도록 [보기]에서 빈칸에 알맞은 것을 골라 문장을 완성하시오. 각 1점

보기	may	may not	can	can't

1 그는 케이크를 만들 수 없다.
   → He _____ make a cake.
2 너희들은 수업 시간에 휴대폰을 사용하면 안 된다.
   → You _____ use your cell phone in class.
3 그 소문은 사실일지도 모른다.
   → The rumor _____ be true.

VOCA repair 수리하다, 고치다 | jump rope 줄넘기 (하다) | across ~을 가로질러 | stream 시내 | take a break 잠깐 쉬다 | rumor 소문, 루머

1 다음 중 밑줄 친 'Can[can]'의 쓰임이 <u>다른</u> 하나는? 2점

　① <u>Can</u> you understand?

　② I <u>can</u> fix my robot.

　③ <u>Can</u> you find the place?

　④ Somebody <u>can</u> help you.

　⑤ <u>Can</u> I use a dictionary on the test?

2 대화의 밑줄 친 우리말을 영어로 바르게 나타낸 것은? 3점

> A: This is my mom's cello.
> B: Wow, can't you play it?
> A: <u>응, 할 수 없어.</u> Only my mom can.

　① Yes, I can.　　② Yes, I can't.　　③ No, I can.

　④ No, I couldn't.　　⑤ No, I can't.

3 How many sentences are grammatically <u>incorrect</u>? 3점

> ⓐ Jiho mays be right.
> ⓑ I can't speak Russian.
> ⓒ Are you able to go with me?
> ⓓ Do you can send email on your phone?
> ⓔ Can he plays with us?

　① one　　② two　　③ three

　④ four　　⑤ five

4 우리말과 일치하도록 빈칸에 알맞은 말을 쓰시오. 4점

> 여기서 사진 찍으시면 안 됩니다.

　→ You _____ take pictures here.

5 다음 문장에서 어법상 어색한 곳을 찾아 바르게 고치시오. 4점

> Jenny may is thirsty. (Jenny는 목이 마를지도 모른다.)

_____ ➡ _____

VOCA　fix 고치다 | dictionary 사전 | Russian 러시아어 | send 보내다 | thirsty 목이 마른

UNIT 12 will, be going to

CONCEPT 1 조동사 will (과거형: would)

조동사 will은 미래와 의지의 뜻을 나타낸다.

	형태	의미	
평서문	will+동사원형	∼할 것이다, ∼하겠다	
부정문	will not[won't]+동사원형	∼하지 않을 것이다, ∼하지 않겠다	
의문문	Will+주어+동사원형 ∼?	대답	Yes, 주어+will. No, 주어+will not[won't].

I will learn fencing someday.

Minho won't agree again.

Will you wait by the door? – Yes, I will. / No, I won't.

줄임말

• 주어와 will을 줄여 쓸 수 있다.

She will → She'll

I will → I'll

They will → They'll

Will/Would you ∼?

• 권유, 부탁을 나타내는 표현이다.

Will you come to my birthday party?

Would you call me back?

CONCEPT 2 be going to

be going to는 가까운 미래나 미리 예정·계획된 일을 나타낸다.

	형태	의미	
평서문	be going to+동사원형	∼할 것이다, ∼할 예정이다	
부정문	be not going to+동사원형	∼하지 않을 것이다	
의문문	Be+주어+going to+동사원형 ∼?	대답	Yes, 주어+be동사. No, 주어+be동사+not.

I am going to meet him soon.

He isn't going to order the keyboard.

Is he going to get a haircut? – Yes, he is. / No, he isn't.

CONCEPT 3 be going to의 여러 가지 뜻

∼할 것이다	∼로 가고 있는 중이다	∼로 갈 것이다
be going to+동사원형	be going to+장소 명사	be going to+장소 명사 +미래 부사(구)

Jamie is going to have lunch. (∼할 것이다)

They are going to the swimming pool now. (∼로 가고 있는 중이다)

He is going to Bali soon. (∼로 갈 것이다)

VOCA fencing 펜싱 | someday (미래) 언젠가 | agree 동의하다 | order 주문하다 | get a haircut 이발하다, 머리를 자르다 | Bali 발리(인도네시아의 섬)

★ Let's Check It Out

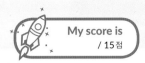

A [ ]에서 알맞은 말을 고르시오. 각 1점

  1 We are going [to visit / visit] our uncle.

  2 Betty [will / wills] play tennis after school.

  3 He will [listen / listens] to English songs from now on.

  4 Bob is going to call her [last night / this evening].

  5 They are going to [be upset / upset].

B 문장을 괄호 안의 지시대로 바꿔 쓰시오. 각 1점

  1 Bora is going to drink Sprite. (부정문)

    ➡ _____

  2 He is going to invite us. (의문문)

    ➡ _____

  3 You will go camping tomorrow. (의문문)

    ➡ _____

  4 They will stay with you. (줄임말 사용)

    ➡ _____

C 대화의 빈칸에 알맞은 대답을 쓰시오. 각 1점

  1 A: Is your brother going to take piano lessons?

    B: _____, _____ _____. He will be a pianist.

  2 A: Will you change your clothes?

    B: _____, _____ _____. I don't have any new clothes.

  3 A: Were you going to invite me?

    B: _____, _____ _____. I really wanted to invite you.

D 밑줄 친 부분의 의미에 유의하여 문장을 해석하시오. 각 1점

  1 The singer is going to sing one more song.

    ➡ _____

  2 They are going to the airport now.

    ➡ _____

  3 He is going to his house soon.

    ➡ _____

VOCA from now on 이제부터 | upset 속상한 | invite 초대하다 | take a lesson 수업을 듣다 | pianist 피아니스트 | clothes 옷

1   빈칸에 들어갈 말로 알맞은 것은? 2점

> We _____ a big festival soon.

① will attend   ② attend   ③ attended
④ were attending   ⑤ don't attend

2   Which is NOT suitable for the blank? 2점

> This advice will be helpful for you _____ .

① someday   ② this time   ③ next week
④ a month ago   ⑤ tomorrow

3   다음 중 어법상 <u>어색한</u> 것으로 묶인 것은? 3점

> ⓐ My friends are going to go to the exhibition.
> ⓑ We are going to be happy.
> ⓒ She is going to late today.
> ⓓ He will go to Paris next week.
> ⓔ Where will they going this Saturday?
> ⓕ They are going to go to Yongsan this evening.

① ⓐ, ⓑ   ② ⓒ, ⓓ, ⓔ   ③ ⓒ, ⓔ
④ ⓑ, ⓒ, ⓓ, ⓕ   ⑤ ⓒ, ⓔ, ⓕ

4   다음은 Terry가 지금 하고 있는 일과 내일 할 일을 나타낸 표이다. 빈칸에 알맞은 말을 각각 <u>3단어</u>로 쓰시오. (단, will은 쓰지 말 것) 4점

Now	Tomorrow
go to the tennis court	go to the park

(1) Terry _____ the tennis court now.

(2) Terry _____ the park tomorrow.

5   Fill in the blanks in the dialog. 4점

> A: Will she take a trip to Europe this summer?
> B: No, _____ _____ . She will stay here.

VOCA   festival 축제 | attend ~에 참석하다 | advice 충고, 조언 | helpful 도움이 되는 | exhibition 전시회 | take a trip 여행 가다

UNIT 13 must, should

CONCEPT 1 조동사 must

뒤에 동사원형이 오고, 의무와 강한 추측의 뜻으로 나눌 수 있다.

		평서문	부정문
의무		must+동사원형: ~해야 한다 (= have/has to)	① 금지: must not+동사원형: ~해서는 안 된다 ② 불필요: don't/doesn't have to+동사원형: ~할 필요가 없다 (= don't need to, need not)
		의문문	대답
		Must+주어+동사원형 ~?	Yes, 주어+must. No, 주어+must not. (금지) No, 주어+don't/doesn't have to. (불필요)
강한 추측		평서문	부정문
		must be: ~임에 틀림없다	cannot[can't] be: ~일 리가 없다

You must come back home.

Kevin doesn't have to get up early on Sunday.

You must not go in a stranger's car.

He must be smart. He can't be foolish.

CONCEPT 2 조동사 should

뒤에 동사원형이 오며, 도덕적 의무나 충고·조언의 뜻을 나타낸다.

	형태	의미	
평서문	should+동사원형 (= ought to)	~해야 한다	
부정문	should not[shouldn't]+동사원형 (= ought not to)	~ 해서는 안 된다	
의문문	Should+주어+동사원형 ~?	대답	Yes, 주어+should. No, 주어+should not [shouldn't].

You should save energy. = You ought to save energy.

We should not waste water. = We ought not to waste water.

Should I lock the door?

– Yes, you should. / No, you shouldn't.

GRAMMAR POINT

must의 의문문

- 「Do/Does+주어+have to+동사원형 ~?」로도 나타낼 수 있다.

  Do I have to call Mom?

  – Yes, you do. / No, you don't.

  What does he have to do?
  (의문사 의문문)

  – He has to apologize.

must(의무)의 과거 표현

- must가 과거의 의무를 나타낼 때 'had to+동사원형'을 쓴다.

- 과거 표현의 부정은 'didn't have to+동사원형'을 쓴다.

  We had to cancel our trip.

  You didn't have to run.

may와 must의 부정의 답

- may not: ~하면 안 된다(금지)

- don't have to = need not:
  ~할 필요 없다(불필요)

  May I go to the bathroom?

  – No, you may not.

  Must I get up early?

  – No, you don't have to.

추측의 강도 비교

- might 〈 may 〈 must

  He might be rich.
  (그는 아마 부자일 것이다.)

  He may be rich.
  (그는 부자일 것이다.)

  He must be rich.
  (그는 부자임에 틀림없다.)

- might not 〈 may not 〈 cannot

  He might not be rich.
  (그는 아마 부자가 아닐 것이다.)

  He may not be rich.
  (그는 부자가 아닐 것이다.)

  He can't be rich.
  (그는 부자일 리가 없다.)

강제성 비교: must 〉 should

- must: 필요에 의한 강제적 의무

- should: 도덕적 의무 및 충고

  We must fasten our seatbelts.

  We should help each other.

VOCA stranger 낯선 사람 | save 절약하다 | waste 낭비하다 | lock 잠그다 | call 부르다, 전화 걸다 | apologize 사과하다

Let's Check It Out

>>> 정답 8쪽

A 우리말과 뜻이 같도록 [ ]에서 알맞은 것을 고르시오. 각 1점

1 나는 언니와 방을 나누어 써야 한다.
→ I [can / must] share a room with my sister.

2 그는 조심해야 한다.
→ He [has to / have to] be careful.

3 Susie는 운동을 더 많이 해야 한다.
→ Susie should [exercise / exercises] more.

4 너는 규칙을 어기면 안 된다.
→ You [must not / don't have to] break the rules.

5 수업 시간에 간식을 먹으면 안 된다.
→ You [ought to not / ought not to] eat snacks in class.

B 문장을 괄호 안의 지시대로 바꾸시오. 각 1점

1 He has to take the trash back home. (의문문)
→ _____

2 Should we reuse the water? (평서문)
→ _____

3 Should I wear a jacket and a tie? (긍정의 대답)
→ _____

C 밑줄 친 부분의 의미를 '의무'와 '추측'으로 구분하시오. 각 1점

1 He <u>must</u> prepare for the party.   → _____

2 She <u>must</u> be proud of you.   → _____

D 괄호 안의 단어들을 알맞게 배열하여 문장을 완성하시오. 각 1점

1 Cinderella (home, return, must, before, midnight).
→ Cinderella _____.

2 We (not, give up, to, ought) hope.
→ We _____ hope.

3 (have, does, take, he, to) his medicine?
→ _____ his medicine?

VOCA share 나누어 쓰다 | careful 조심하는 | exercise 운동하다 | break a rule 규칙을 어기다 | trash 쓰레기 | reuse 재사용하다 | prepare 준비하다 | be proud of ~을 자랑스러워하다 | midnight 자정 | give up 포기하다

My score is

Let's Check It Out _____ / 13점   0~17점 → Level 1 Test
Ready for Exams _____ / 12점 → 18~21점 → Level 2 Test
Total _____ / 25점   22~25점 → Level 3 Test

>>> 정답 9쪽

1   Which is proper for the blank? 2점

> She _____ play for our team. We really need her.

① need not   ② must   ③ must not
④ doesn't have to   ⑤ have to

2   다음 중 밑줄 친 'must'의 의미가 다른 하나는? 2점

① You <u>must</u> understand yourself.

② He <u>must</u> be American.

③ Oh, I <u>must</u> sit down for a minute.

④ She <u>must</u> go back to New York tonight.

⑤ I <u>must</u> finish this work by noon.

3   다음 중 어법상 어색한 것으로 묶인 것은? 2점

> ⓐ You not must stay here.
> ⓑ You must to stop at the red light.
> ⓒ Where do I must park my car?
> ⓓ You don't have to buy candles.
> ⓔ You should read more books.

① ⓐ, ⓑ, ⓒ   ② ⓐ, ⓑ, ⓔ   ③ ⓑ, ⓔ
④ ⓑ, ⓒ, ⓓ   ⑤ ⓑ, ⓓ, ⓔ

4   밑줄 친 표현과 바꿔 쓸 수 있는 말을 3단어로 쓰시오. 3점

> You <u>should not</u> make any noise in public places.

→ _____ _____ _____

5   Fill in the blank with 3 words. 3점

> It was a national holiday yesterday, so I _____
> go to school.

VOCA   American 미국의; 미국인(의) | make noise 소란을 부리다, 시끄럽게 하다 | public place 공공장소 | national holiday 국경일, 공휴일

64

CHAPTER 04
Review Test

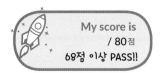

My score is
/ 80점
68점 이상 PASS!!

>>> 정답 9쪽

U11_3

01 다음 중 밑줄 친 'May[may]'의 뜻이 다른 하나는? 2점

① You <u>may</u> leave earlier.
② It <u>may</u> rain tomorrow.
③ <u>May</u> I help you?
④ <u>May</u> I take a look at your notebook?
⑤ You <u>may</u> turn on the TV.

U11_2+GP

02 Which is suitable for the blank? 2점

> I am able to cook Korean food very well.
> = I _____ cook Korean food very well.

① may   ② must
③ can   ④ will
⑤ do

U12_1+GP

03 다음 중 밑줄 친 부분이 어법상 어색한 것은? 2점

① I'll <u>read</u> easy English books.
② What <u>will you do</u> this weekend?
③ He <u>will meet not</u> her.
④ She <u>won't cry</u> again.
⑤ <u>Will</u> Tom and Jerry <u>fight</u> again?

U13_1

04 다음 중 문장의 의미가 서로 다른 것은? 2점

함정

① You have to go now.
   = You must go now.
② They need not come here early.
   = They don't have to come here early.
③ She must not cross here.
   = She doesn't have to cross here.
④ He has to save money for the future.
   = He must save money for the future.
⑤ We don't have to help him.
   = We don't need to help him.

U13_1+GP

05 다음 중 어법상 옳은 문장을 모두 고르시오. 3점

★
고난도

① Do we must give him some money?
② He wasn't able to climb the tree.
③ They have to go to the store for some drinks.
④ I don't have to meet him yesterday.
⑤ He won't be late again.

U13_1

06 내용상 빈칸에 이어질 말로 적당한 것은? 2점

> Susan doesn't look well. _____.

① She must be sick
② She must be rich
③ She must work harder
④ She can't be sick
⑤ She doesn't have to lose weight

U13_2

07 다음 대화의 빈칸에 알맞은 말을 고르시오. 2점

> A: I want to see a motor show tomorrow.
>   What should I do?
> B: You _____ make a reservation on the
>   Internet.

① must not   ② will
③ can't   ④ are going to
⑤ should

U13_2

08 Which has the same meaning as the following sentence? 2점

> Please be quiet in the book café.

① You don't be quiet in the book café.
② You need not be quiet in the book café.
③ You should be quiet in the book café.
④ You will be quiet in the book café.
⑤ You has to be quiet in the book café.

09 빈칸에 들어갈 단어를 바르게 쓰지 <u>못한</u> 학생은? 2점

I won't call him _____.

① 민지: tomorrow
② 호준: this afternoon
③ 재민: next week
④ 영민: tonight
⑤ 소라: last week

10 다음 중 밑줄 친 'must'의 쓰임이 <u>다른</u> 하나는? 2점

① She <u>must</u> go home.
② He <u>must</u> be tired.
③ The kid <u>must</u> be nervous.
④ His dog <u>must</u> be smart.
⑤ It <u>must</u> be rainy.

11 ★ 고난도 Which sentence is grammatically <u>wrong</u>? (Up to 3 answers) 3점

① You guys should careful.
② You're going to hurt yourself.
③ You should ask for the reason first.
④ I won't to be nervous.
⑤ Are you able to going up two flights of stairs?

12 ★ 고난도 다음 중 어법상 옳은 문장은 모두 몇 개인가? 3점

ⓐ Can you give advice to your children?
ⓑ She doesn't has to buy any eggs.
ⓒ The boys aren't going to tell your secret.
ⓓ Ben does not have to working tomorrow.
ⓔ Are Tom and Wendy going to take pictures?
ⓕ Is Wendy playing the piano yesterday?

① 0개   ② 1개
③ 2개   ④ 3개
⑤ 4개

13 ★ 고난도 Which set CANNOT make a grammatically correct sentence? 4점

① can / you / an / electric / ride / kickboard / ?
② you / ? / volunteer / are / able / to / with / him
③ may / you / not / went / first / .
④ do / have / to / finish / ? / the project / you
⑤ we / to / . / ought / save / energy

14 함정 다음 중 어법상 <u>어색한</u> 문장으로 짝지어진 것은? 2점

ⓐ You should be proud of yourselves.
ⓑ You ought to not behave rudely.
ⓒ She must be selfish.
ⓓ He can't be rich.
ⓔ He don't have to wake up early.

① ⓐ, ⓑ   ② ⓐ, ⓒ
③ ⓑ, ⓓ   ④ ⓑ, ⓔ
⑤ ⓒ, ⓔ

15 How many grammatical errors are there? 2점

ⓐ Mr. Lee have to finish the research.
ⓑ She musts not late for the meeting.

① one   ② two
③ three   ④ four
⑤ five

16 대화의 빈칸에 들어갈 말로 문맥상 <u>어색한</u> 것은? 2점

A: Must I contact her only through email?
B: _____.

① Yes, you must
② No, you must not
③ No, you don't have to
④ No, you need not
⑤ Yes, you have to

17 U11_2+3
두 문장이 같은 의미가 되도록 빈칸에 알맞은 말을 쓰시오. 3점

> Can I ask just one quick question?

→ _____ I ask just one quick question?

18 U11_2
대화의 빈칸에 알맞은 말을 쓰시오. (1단어) 4점

> Mina: Can you play the violin?
> John: Yes. I _____ play the violin before, but I can now.

19 U13_2
밑줄 친 부분과 같은 의미인 것을 <u>모두</u> 고르시오. 4점

> You <u>should not</u> talk to strangers.
>
> ⓐ don't need to　　ⓑ ought not to
> ⓒ can't　　　　　　ⓓ won't
> ⓔ don't have to　　ⓕ need not
> ⓖ are not going to

→ _____

20 U13_GP
추측의 강도에 따라 문장을 완성하시오. (각 2단어) 각 2점

> 100% → She is smart.
> 90% → She _____ smart.
> 50% → She _____ smart.
> 10% → She _____ smart.
> 0% → She isn't smart.

21 U13_1+2+GP
Look at the picture and fill in the blank with <u>1 word</u>. 3점

→ You _____ be quiet in the library.

22 U11_2
두 문장이 같은 의미가 되도록 빈칸에 알맞은 말을 쓰시오. 4점

> You can't count up to one hundred million.

→ You _____ _____ _____ to count up to one hundred million.

23 U11_3+U13_1
빈칸에 알맞은 말을 쓰시오. (2단어) 4점

> Janitor: Excuse me, sir. You _____ _____ smoke here. It's against the rules. Didn't you see the sign?
>
> *janitor: 건물 관리인　**against: ~에 어긋나서

24 U13_GP
Complete the question for the following answer. (5 words) 5점

> Q: What _____?
> A: He has to wear a suit.

25 U12_2
조건에 맞게 우리말을 영작하시오. 6점

> 우리는 그녀를 만날 건가요?
> ·조건 1　go, meet을 반드시 쓸 것
> ·조건 2　6단어로 쓸 것

→ _____

26 U13_1+GP
대화가 자연스러운 의미가 되도록 빈칸을 채우시오. 4점

> A: Do I have to clean my room, Mom?
> B: No, you _____. I already cleaned it this morning. But the next time, you must do it by yourself.

한눈에 쏙! 아래 노트를 보면서 빈칸을 채워 보세요.

1 조동사의 형태

조동사 **+** 1) _____

2 바꾸어 쓸 수 있는 표현

can	= be 1) _____ to (~할 수 있다)
will	= be 2) _____ to (~할 것이다)
★ must	= have/has to (3) _____)
must not	= 4) _____ _____ = cannot (~하면 안 된다)
need not	= 5) _____ / _____ _____ _____ (~할 필요 없다)
should not	= ought 6) _____ _____ (~하면 안 된다)

3 be going to의 여러 가지 뜻

* I am going to go to school. (~할 것이다) = will
  → +동사원형
* I am going to school. (~로 가고 있는 중이다)
  → +장소
* I am going to school soon. (1) _____)
  → +미래 부사

헷갈리지 말자! 초록색으로 표시된 부분을 바르게 고쳐 쓰세요.

1 He will <u>can</u> win first prize.
   └→

2 <u>Must</u> she have to call her mom?
   └→

CHAPTER 05
문장의 변환

14 의문사 의문문

CONCEPT 1 의문사

육하원칙(누가, 무엇을, 언제, 어디서, 어떻게, 왜)을 묻는 말을 의문사라 한다.

의문사	뜻	묻는 것
who	누가	사람의 이름, 신분, 가족 관계
what	무엇; 어떤	사물 또는 사람의 직업
when	언제	시간, 때
where	어디서	장소
why	왜	이유
how	어떻게, 얼마나	방법, 수단, 상태

Who is that tall woman? – She's my English teacher.

What did you do last night? – I watched a baseball game.

When is your birthday? – It's on November 27.

Where does the show take place? – It takes place at Seoul Square.

Why do you like me? – You're a nice person.

How did you come in? – The door was open.

CONCEPT 2 주의해야 할 의문사

의문사	뜻	사용
whom	누구를	목적격일 때(who를 써도 됨)
whose	누구의 (것)	소유를 물을 때
which	어느 (것), 어떤 (것)	선택을 물을 때
how+형용사/부사	얼마나 ~	정도를 물을 때

Who(m) do you like the most in your class?

Whose shoes are they? – They're my cousin's.

Which is yours, this or that? – That is mine.

How far is the far-faraway kingdom?

CONCEPT 3 의문사 의문문의 어순

be동사	의문사+be동사+주어 ~?
일반동사	의문사+do/does/did+주어+동사원형 ~?

Who is absent today? – Nobody's absent today.

What do you want? – I want a banana latte.

GRAMMAR POINT

what time

- 구체적인 시간을 물을 때는 what time을 사용한다.

  What time do you close today?

의문대명사와 의문형용사

- what, whose, which는 의문대명사로 사용되거나 명사를 수식하는 의문형용사로 사용된다.

  What do you want to get for your birthday? (의문대명사)

  What kind of dance do you like? (의문형용사)

  Whose laptop is this? (의문형용사)

  Whose is that car? (의문대명사)

  Which is your hat? (의문대명사)

  Which way is out? (의문형용사)

what과 which

- what은 막연한 대상에, which는 정해진 대상에 사용한다.

  What is your wish?

  Which do you like better, summer or winter?

의문사 의문문에 대한 대답

- 의문사로 시작하는 의문문에는 Yes/ No로 대답하지 않는다.

Why don't you ~?

- '~하는 게 어때?'의 의미로 권유를 나타낸다.

  Why don't you come in?

의문사가 주어일 때의 어순

- 의문사가 주어이며 동사가 일반동사인 경우는 「의문사+동사+목적어 ~?」로 쓴다.

  Who taught you?

  – Yoda taught me.

VOCA take place 일어나다, 열리다 | far 먼 | kingdom 왕국 | absent 결석한

Let's Check It Out

>>> 정답 10쪽

A [ ]에서 알맞은 것을 고르시오. 각 1점

1 [Who / Whose] mother is she?

2 [Whom / Which] character in the game is your favorite?

3 [What / Where] do you buy your clothes?

4 [When / What] does he come here?

5 [Why / How] are you angry?

B 빈칸에 알맞은 의문사를 쓰시오. 각 1점

1 너는 누구를 초대했니?

→ _____ did you invite?

2 넌 어느 팀을 좋아하니, Dragons니 Dogs니?

→ _____ team do you like, the Dragons or the Dogs?

3 이 컴퓨터는 얼마나 오래되었니?

→ _____ old is this computer?

C 대화의 빈칸에 알맞은 의문사를 쓰시오. 각 1점

1 A: _____ hula hoop is that?

B: It belongs to Sophia.

2 A: _____ tall is he?

B: He is 183 centimeters tall.

3 A: _____ are you free?

B: I'm free on Monday.

D 주어진 단어를 바르게 배열하여 <u>의문문을 만드시오</u>. 각 1점

1 her phone case, color, what, is

→ _____

2 leave, she, why, did, early

→ _____

3 my, moved, cheese, who

→ _____

VOCA character 등장인물 | hula hoop 훌라후프 | belong to ~에 속하다, ~의 것이다 | free 한가한 | move 옮기다

My score is

Let's Check It Out _____ / 14점   0~20점 → Level 1 Test
Ready for Exams _____ / 16점 ➡ 21~25점 → Level 2 Test
Total _____ / 30점   26~30점 → Level 3 Test

>>> 정답 10쪽

1 Which answer is correct for the question? 2점

A: What do you have for breakfast?
B: _____

① Yes, I do.   ② No, I don't.   ③ I'm very hungry.
④ I don't like rice.   ⑤ I just have an apple.

2 각 빈칸에 들어갈 말이 바르게 짝지어진 것은? 3점

• _____ is that girl?
• _____ do you like better, beef or pork?

① Who – Which   ② What – Which   ③ Who – What
④ What – Who   ⑤ Which – What

3 다음 대화 중 어색한 것은? 3점

① What's your first name? – It's Hyeyun.
② Who is she? – She is my neighbor.
③ What's that in your hand? – It's a ring.
④ What do you do? – I work out.
⑤ When does he come back? – In 30 minutes.

4 Look at the picture and complete the question. 4점

A: _____ does it _____?
B: It means good luck.

5 다음 빈칸에 공통으로 들어갈 단어를 쓰시오. 4점

• _____ can I get to the museum?
• _____ is the weather in Moscow?
• _____ long do you stay in school?

➡ _____

VOCA beef 소고기 | pork 돼지고기 | neighbor 이웃 | work out 운동하다 | mean 의미하다 | Moscow 모스크바(러시아의 수도) | museum 박물관

UNIT 15 명령문

CONCEPT 1 명령문

상대방에게 명령, 부탁, 요청 등을 표현할 때 명령문을 사용한다.

A 긍정 명령문과 부정 명령문

	어순	해석
긍정 명령문	동사원형 ~.	~해라.
부정 명령문	Don't[Do not] 동사원형 ~.	~하지 마라.

You are kind. → Be kind.

You stay there alone. → Don't stay there alone.

You go out at night. → Do not go out at night.

B Let's 청유문

'~하자' 또는 '~하지 말자'라고 제안할 때 사용한다.

	어순	해석
긍정 청유문	Let's + 동사원형 ~.	~하자.
부정 청유문	Let's not + 동사원형 ~.	~하지 말자.

Let's have dinner now.

Let's not blame him.

GRAMMAR POINT

never 부정 명령문

• 부정 명령문을 강조하기 위해 never를 쓸 수도 있다.

You do that again.

→ Never do that again.

please

• 명령문 앞이나 뒤에 please를 붙이면 좀 더 부드럽고 정중한 표현이 된다.

Help me, please.

Please come again.

Let's 청유문에 대한 대답

• Let's 청유문에 대한 긍정과 부정의 대답은 Yes, let's. 또는 No, let's not.으로 한다.

Let's watch this movie.

– Yes, let's.

Let's not go to the singing room.

– No, let's not.

let + 목적어 + 동사원형

• 「let + 목적어 + 동사원형」은 '(목적어)가 ~하게 해주세요'의 의미로 사용된다.

Let me go home.

(집에 가게 해주세요.)

Let her cry.

(그녀가 울게 놔둬.)

VOCA blame 비난하다 | singing room 노래방

Let's Check It Out

>>> 정답 10쪽

A [ ]에서 알맞은 것을 고르시오. 각 1점

1 [Not / Don't] be shy.
2 [Cut / Cutting] the red ribbon.
3 [Puts / Put] your hands up.
4 [Never / Not] give up.

B 다음 빈칸에 알맞은 말을 쓰시오. 각 1점

1 같이 노래합시다.
   → _____ _____ along.

2 시간을 낭비하지 맙시다.
   → _____ _____ _____ time.

3 친구가 됩시다.
   → _____ _____ friends.

C 다음을 괄호 안의 지시대로 바꿔 쓰시오. 각 1점

1 You fasten your seatbelt. (긍정 명령문)
   → _____

2 You're too proud. (부정 명령문)
   → _____

3 You're angry. (부정 명령문)
   → _____

D 밑줄 친 부분을 바르게 고쳐 쓰시오. 각 1점

1 Let me holding your hand.   → _____
2 Never did this again.   → _____
3 Not swim here.   → _____
4 Let's joins the comic book club. → _____
5 Not let's think about it now.   → _____

VOCA shy 수줍은, 부끄러운 | give up 포기하다 | waste 낭비하다 | fasten 조이다, 잠그다, 채우다 | seatbelt 안전 벨트 | proud 자부심이 강한, 자랑스러워하는

74

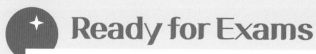

My score is

Let's Check It Out _____ / 15점   0~17점 → Level 1 Test
Ready for Exams _____ / 10점   ➡   18~21점 → Level 2 Test
Total _____ / 25점   22~25점 → Level 3 Test

Ready for Exams

>>> 정답 10쪽

---

1 다음 빈칸에 알맞은 것은? 2점

| _____ a gentleman. |

① Do   ② Does   ③ Are

④ Is   ⑤ Be

---

2 Which is grammatically <u>incorrect</u>? 2점

① Let him kick the ball.

② Please don't close the window.

③ Let's took a break for 5 minutes.

④ Don't put your finger in your nose.

⑤ Let's not wear ties on Fridays.

---

3 그림을 보고 괄호 안의 단어를 이용해서 엄마가 딸에게 할 수 있는 말을 완성하시오. 3점

→ Go and _____ _____ _____! (wash)

---

4 Complete the sign according to the conditions. 3점

·Condition 1	부정 명령문을 사용할 것
·Condition 2	touch를 포함시킬 것
·Condition 3	3단어로 쓸 것

→ _____

VOCA   gentleman 신사 | tie 넥타이

UNIT

1 부가의문문

평서문 뒤에, 상대방의 동의를 구하거나 사실을 확인하기 위해 붙이는 의문문으로 '그렇지?' 또는 '그렇지 않니?' 등으로 해석한다.

A 부가의문문 만들기

형태	긍정 → 부정
	부정 → 긍정
동사	be동사/조동사 → 그대로
	일반동사 → do/does/did로

The babies are cute, aren't they?

He can't even cook ramen, can he?

She hates fish, doesn't she?

We missed a great show, didn't we?

B 명령문과 Let's 청유문의 부가의문문

명령문	~, will you?
Let's 청유문	~, shall we?

Hurry home, will you?

Let's go for a walk, shall we?

GRAMMAR POINT

부가의문문의 주어

• 부가의문문의 주어는 대명사로 쓴다.

  Scott feels thirsty, doesn't he?

  This isn't very good, is it?

there is 구문의 부가의문문

• there가 주어는 아니지만 부가의문문에서는 주어 역할을 한다.

  There is something wrong, isn't there?

부정 명령문의 부가의문문

• 부정문에서도 부가의문문은 will you?나 shall we?를 쓴다.

  Don't say a word, will you?

  Let's not finish this today, shall we?

VOCA even 심지어, ~조차 | ramen 라면 | miss 놓치다 | go for a walk 산책을 가다 | thirsty 목이 마른 | finish 끝내다

A [ ]에서 알맞은 것을 고르시오. 각 1점

1 You aren't happy today, [aren't / are] you?

2 He was at home, [wasn't / was] he?

3 Sam lay down in bed all day, [didn't / did] he?

4 She can't beat you at the game, [can't / can] she?

5 Pass me the salt, [don't / will] you?

B [보기]에서 빈칸에 알맞은 표현을 골라 쓰시오. 각 1점

| 보기 | can he | doesn't he | isn't she | won't they | are you |

1 You aren't tired, _____?

2 Eric plays soccer, _____?

3 The aliens will invade us, _____?

4 She is strong and beautiful, _____?

5 He can't run up the hill, _____?

C 밑줄 친 부분을 바르게 고치시오. 각 1점

1 Min and Jin are sisters, <u>are they</u>?　→ _____

2 You weren't present, <u>weren't you</u>?　→ _____

3 She won't stay with us, <u>doesn't she</u>?　→ _____

4 David, lock the door, <u>doesn't he</u>?　→ _____

5 Let's go to the Internet café, <u>will you</u>?　→ _____

D 빈칸에 알맞은 부가의문문을 쓰시오. 각 1점

1 That was awesome, _____?

2 We hated each other, _____?

3 Please help him, _____?

4 The man took the pills, _____?

5 Let's not take this way, _____?

VOCA lie down 눕다 | beat 이기다 | alien 외계인 | invade 침략[침입]하다 | present 출석한 | lock 잠그다 | awesome 굉장한 | pill 알약

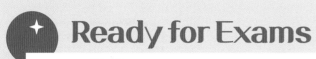
🚀 **My score is**

Let's Check It Out _____ / 20점   0~24점 → Level 1 Test
Ready for Exams _____ / 15점   ➡   25~29점 → Level 2 Test
Total _____ / 35점   30~35점 → Level 3 Test

1 다음 대화의 빈칸에 알맞은 것은? 2점

> A: The exam was very easy, _____?
> B: No, it wasn't. It was difficult for me.

① was it   ② did it   ③ wasn't it

④ didn't it   ⑤ wasn't the exam

2 Which is correct for the blank? 2점

> Chunhyang, look at me, _____?

① aren't you   ② are you   ③ will you

④ do you   ⑤ doesn't she

3 다음 중 어법상 옳은 것을 <u>모두</u> 고르시오. 3점

① Let me go, shall we?
② They will come back, won't they?
③ There aren't many people today, are they?
④ Let's meet at the square, shall we?
⑤ She doesn't eat kimchi, does she?

4 그림을 보고 조건에 맞도록 대화문의 빈칸 (A)와 (B)에 알맞은 말을 쓰시오. 4점

> A: Mari is a nurse, ____(A)____?
> B: ____(B)____. She's a doctor.
>
> ·조건 I   부가의문문을 사용할 것
> ·조건 2   (A)는 2단어, (B)는 3단어로 쓸 것

(A) _____

(B) _____

5 Translate the sentence. Use the given word. 4점

> 그는 웹툰을 좋아하지, 그렇지 않니? (webtoons)

→ _____

VOCA   exam 시험 | square 광장 | webtoon 웹툰

78

감탄문

1 감탄문

감탄문은 기쁨, 슬픔, 놀라움 등의 감정을 표현하는 문장으로 '참[정말] ~하구나!'로 해석한다.

A What 감탄문

감탄의 대상	어순
명사	What+(a/an)+형용사+명사 (+주어+동사)!

It is a very fast car. → What a fast car (it is)!

That is a very big full moon. → What a big full moon (that is)!

She has a very clever cat. → What a clever cat she has!

B How 감탄문

감탄의 대상	어순
형용사 또는 부사	How+형용사/부사 (+주어+동사)!

He is very cute. → How cute (he is)!

Your legs are so long. → How long your legs are!

Your brother runs very fast. → How fast your brother runs!

GRAMMAR POINT

감탄문에서 부정관사의 사용

• 단수 명사가 있는 모음 앞에서는 an을 쓰고, 복수 명사인 경우는 a 나 an을 쓰지 않는다.

It was a very exciting game.
→ What an exciting game it was!

They have very cute dogs.
→ What cute dogs they have!

두 가지 감탄문 만들기

• 강조하는 대상을 달리하여 what 과 how로 시작하는 두 가지 감탄 문을 만들 수 있다.

You are a very smart girl.
→ girl(명사) 감탄: What a smart girl you are!
→ smart(형용사) 감탄: How smart you are!

VOCA full moon 보름달 | clever 영리한 | exciting 흥미진진한

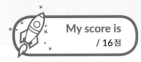
A [ ]에서 알맞은 것을 고르시오. 각 1점

1 [What / How] selfish you are!

2 [What / How] a cool man he is!

3 [What / How] positive she is!

4 [What / How] brave boys they were!

B 빈칸에 'What'과 'How' 중 알맞은 것을 쓰시오. 각 1점

1 _____ an amazing story it is!

2 _____ old the picture is!

3 _____ a fast train the KTX is!

4 _____ pretty flowers you planted!

C 문장을 감탄문으로 바꿀 때 빈칸에 알맞은 말을 쓰시오. 각 1점

1 The room is very large.

→ _____ _____ the room is!

2 I was so pleased.

→ _____ _____ I was!

3 She is a very strange girl.

→ _____ _____ _____ _____ she is!

4 It is very clean water.

→ _____ _____ _____ it is!

D 문장에서 <u>어색한</u> 부분을 찾아 바르게 고치시오. 각 1점

1 How an exciting place it is!

_____ → _____

2 What gentle the wind is!

_____ → _____

3 What a boring people they are!

_____ → _____

4 What slowly the traffic moves!

_____ → _____

VOCA **selfish** 이기적인 | **positive** 긍정적인 | **brave** 용감한 | **amazing** 놀라운 | **plant** 심다 | **pleased** 기쁜 | **strange** 이상한 | **gentle** 온화한 | **boring** 지루한 | **traffic** 차량들, 교통량 | **move** 움직이다

80

Ready for Exams

>>> 정답 11쪽

My score is

Let's Check It Out _____ / 16점   0~17점 → Level 1 Test
Ready for Exams _____ / 9점 → 18~21점 → Level 2 Test
Total _____ / 25점   22~25점 → Level 3 Test

1   다음 각 빈칸에 알맞은 말이 바르게 짝지어진 것은? 2점

> • _____ scary the bear was!
>
> • _____ a tall building it is!

① How – Which   ② How – What   ③ Why – What

④ What – What   ⑤ What – How

2   다음 우리말을 영어로 바르게 옮긴 학생은? 2점

> 너 정말 웃긴 애구나!

① 수지: What funny kid you are!

② 경민: How funny kid you are!

③ 한솔: How a funny kid you are!

④ 규민: What a funny kid are you!

⑤ 다은: What a funny kid you are!

3   다음 중 어법상 <u>어색한</u> 것을 고르시오. 2점

① How dirty your shirt is!

② How cute your brother is!

③ What an old car you have!

④ What interesting books they are!

⑤ What fast computer you have!

4   Find ALL of the errors and rewrite the sentence correctly. 3점

> What excited were the players!

→ _____

VOCA   scary 무서운 | excited 신이 난 | player 선수

UNIT **17**   81

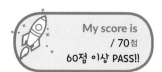

>>> 정답 11쪽

U14_GP

01 다음 질문에 대한 답으로 알맞은 것은? 2점

> A: What time does the movie start?
> B: _____ .

① It's very boring
② Today isn't Friday
③ I don't like the movie
④ You can watch it anytime
⑤ It begins in about 20 minutes

U14_1

02 Which dialog is unnatural? 2점

① A: What's on the table?
  B: My bag.
② A: Who is that boy over there?
  B: Oh, that boy? He is my cousin.
③ A: What class do you like?
  B: My favorite class is P.E.
④ A: What's that in your hand?
  B: It's an action figure.
⑤ A: What's your favorite color?
  B: Red makes me hungry.

U15_1B

03 다음 빈칸에 알맞은 것은? 2점

> Let's _____ the roller coaster.

① takes   ② not take
③ took   ④ takes not
⑤ don't take

U15_1A

04 다음 문장을 바르게 고친 학생은? 2점

> Don't be visit the castle at night.

① 선희: Don't be the castle at night.
② 설아: Don't visits the castle at night.
③ 민준: Doesn't be the castle at night.
④ 찬영: Do visit not the castle at night.
⑤ 채니: Don't visit the castle at night.

U16_1

05 다음 중 밑줄 친 부분이 어법상 올바른 것은? 3점

① The program is not fun anymore, <u>isn't it</u>?
② Julie goes to the gym every day, <u>does she</u>?
③ Your sister can drive a car, <u>can't you</u>?
④ Never copy your friend's homework, <u>will you</u>?
⑤ Let's go to Dubai for the summer, <u>don't we</u>?

U16_1

06 각 빈칸에 들어갈 말이 바르게 짝지어진 것은? 3점

> • Let me pick you up there, _____ ?
> • Lisa didn't order anything, _____ ?

① shall we – didn't she
② shall we – didn't Lisa
③ don't you – did she
④ will you – did she
⑤ will you – did Lisa

U17_1

07 빈칸에 적절하지 않은 것을 모두 고르시오. 2점

> What a(n) _____ !

① old tree it is
② big your son is
③ clever is she
④ wonderful world is it
⑤ comfortable beds they have

U17_1

08 다음 중 어법상 옳은 것으로 묶인 것은? 4점

> ⓐ What a cute mice!
> ⓑ How noisy you are!
> ⓒ How a big screen it is!
> ⓓ How beautiful your mom was!
> ⓔ What a amazing app you have!
> ⓕ What interesting books these are!

① ⓐ, ⓒ   ② ⓐ, ⓑ, ⓔ
③ ⓑ, ⓓ, ⓕ   ④ ⓒ, ⓔ
⑤ ⓓ, ⓕ

09 U16_1B
주어진 단어와 구두점을 조건에 맞게 배열하시오. 4점

> · 조건 1   줄임말을 쓰지 말 것
> · 조건 2   대소문자를 바르게 고쳐 쓸 것
> ----
> you / come / again / , / do / will / not / ?

→ _____

10 U14_1+3
다음과 같은 대답이 나올 수 있도록 조건에 맞는 질문을 영어로 쓰시오. 5점

> My favorite subject is ethics.
> ----
> · 조건 1   위 문장에 있는 단어를 2개 이상 사용할 것
> · 조건 2   5단어로 쓸 것

→ _____

11 U14_2+3

다음 주어진 단어들을 배열하여 의문문을 쓰시오. 5점

> many, in, teachers, there, your, how, are, school

→ _____

12 U15_1A
One of the two sentences has an error. Correct the error. 4점

> ⓐ Jason, please don't breaks your promise.
> ⓑ Girls, be proud of yourselves!

(   ) _____ → _____

13 U15_1A
Look at the picture and complete the sentence. 4점

→ It's the police! _____!
(put ~ down, the gun)

14 U16_1A
다음 문장의 빈칸에 알맞은 부가의문문을 쓰시오. 4점

> McClane, you will come and save me,
> _____?

15 U16_1A
어법상 어색한 것을 찾아 바르게 고치시오. 4점

> Clara threw out the first ball at the baseball game, wasn't she?

→ _____ → _____

16 U16_1A
Translate the underlined sentences into English. 각 4점
함정

> A: She won't come, (A)그렇지?
> B: (B)아니, 올 거야.

(A) _____
(B) _____

17 U17_1B
주어진 단어 중 필요한 것만 골라 감탄문을 만드시오. 6점

> does, how, she, fluently, what, English, speaks

→ _____

18 U17_1A
다음은 문장 해석 숙제를 번역기로 돌린 것이다. 주어진 영어 문장을 우리말로 바르게 해석하시오. 6점

→ _____

시험 직전에 챙겨 보는 **비법 노트**

한눈에 쏙! 아래 노트를 보면서 빈칸을 채워 보세요.

1 의문사 의문문

- 의문사+be동사+1)_____ ~?

- 의문사+do/2)_____/3)_____+주어+4)_____ ~?

2 명령문

	긍정	부정
명령문	1)_____ ~.	Don't+2)_____ ~.
Let's ~	3)_____+4)_____ ~.	Let's 5)_____+6)_____ ~.

3 부가의문문

	be동사	조동사	일반동사
평서문	~, be동사+1)_____? (긍정↔부정)	~, 2)_____+주어? (긍정↔부정)	긍정문, don't/doesn't/3)_____+4)_____? 부정문, do/5)_____/did+6)_____?
명령문	~, 7)_____ _____? → 부정 명령문도! ☆		
Let's ~	~, 8)_____ _____? → Let's not도!		

4 감탄문

→ 명사가 복수형이면 생략

- What (ə[ən])+1)_____+2)_____ (+주어+동사)!

- How+3)_____/4)_____ (+주어+동사)!

헷갈리지 말자! 초록색으로 표시된 부분을 바르게 고쳐 쓰세요.

1 Please don't be come again.

2 What a big fish they are!

CHAPTER 06

형용사와 부사

UNIT 18 형용사

CONCEPT 1 형용사의 의미와 용법

형용사는 명사를 직접 꾸며주거나 주어의 상태를 간접적으로 나타낸다.

A **한정적 용법**: 형용사가 뒤의 명사를 직접 꾸며준다.

She is a kind girl.

B **서술적 용법**: 형용사가 주어로 쓰인 명사나 대명사를 간접적으로 꾸며준다.

The man is very strong.

GRAMMAR POINT

-one, -body, -thing

- -one, -body, -thing으로 끝나는 대명사는 형용사가 뒤에서 꾸며준다.

  I just saw something strange.

CONCEPT 2 수량 형용사

수(셀 수 있는 명사)나 양(셀 수 없는 명사)을 나타내는 형용사를 말한다.

	많은		약간의	조금의	거의 없는
수	many	a lot of, lots of, plenty of	some(긍정문, 권유문) any(부정문, 의문문)	a few	few
양	much			a little	little

They raise many pigs on the farm.   I don't have much money now.

He knows a few Chinese words.   We had little luck in the last game.

some과 any

- some은 긍정문과 권유문에, any는 부정문과 의문문에 쓰인다. 의문문이어도 권유의 의미일 때는 some을 쓴다.

  He wants to eat some food.
  Would you like some coffee?
  She doesn't have any time.
  Do you have any coins?

CONCEPT 3 기수와 서수

기수는 개수를 나타내고, 서수는 순서를 나타낸다.

A **서수 만드는 법**

1, 2, 3	first, second, third
대부분+-th	fourth, sixth
-e → -e 빼고 -th	nine → ninth
-ve → ve를 f로 바꾸고+-th	five → fifth, twelve → twelfth
-ty → y를 ie로 바꾸고+-th	twenty → twentieth

B **기수와 서수의 예**

• one → first	• seven → seventh	• thirteen → thirteenth
• two → second	• eight → eighth	• twenty → twentieth
• three → third	• nine → ninth	• thirty → thirtieth
• four → fourth	• ten → tenth	• hundred → hundredth
• five → fifth	• eleven → eleventh	• thousand → thousandth
• six → sixth	• twelve → twelfth	• million → millionth

-st, -nd, -rd, -th

- 숫자를 그대로 쓰고 뒤에 -st, -nd, -rd, -th를 붙여 서수를 나타낼 수도 있다.

  1st, 2nd, 3rd, 4th... 11th, 12th, 13th... 21st, 22nd, 23rd...

  I'm in the 1st grade.
  They live on the 3rd floor.

VOCA   raise 기르다, 키우다 | luck 운 | coin 동전 | grade 학년

Let's Check It Out

정답 12쪽

A 밑줄 친 형용사가 [보기]에서와 용법이 같으면 =로, 아니면 ≠로 표시하시오. 각 1점

> **보기** He is <u>bad</u> at math.

1 Was it <u>helpful</u>? → _____

2 He did a <u>good</u> job. → _____

3 This is a <u>slow</u> train. → _____

4 He is a <u>funny</u> teacher. → _____

5 Your dog is <u>hungry</u>. → _____

B 밑줄 친 부분을 바르게 고쳐 쓰시오. 각 1점

1 He took <u>much</u> pictures. → _____

2 Do you get <u>many</u> rain in summer? → _____

3 This car needs <u>lot of</u> gas. → _____

4 We met <u>a little</u> famous artists. → _____

5 I had <u>few</u> trouble with them. → _____

C [   ]에서 알맞은 것을 고르시오. 각 1점

1 Do you have [some / any] questions?

2 She sold [some / any] cool clothes online.

3 I don't see [some / any] stars now.

4 The monkey grabbed [some / any] food.

5 Would you like [some / any] more juice?

D 괄호 안에 주어진 숫자를 서수로 쓰시오. (알파벳으로 쓸 것) 각 1점

1 My _____ song was a big hit. (1)

2 It is his _____ birthday. (2)

3 He is in the _____ grade. (9)

4 Our team came in _____ place. (11)

5 I was born on April _____ . (30)

VOCA gas 휘발유 | trouble 문제, 어려움 | grab 움켜쥐다 | hit 히트 곡

My score is

Let's Check It Out _____ / 20점   0~20점 → Level 1 Test
Ready for Exams _____ / 10점   ➡️ 21~25점 → Level 2 Test
Total _____ / 30점   26~30점 → Level 3 Test

Ready for Exams

››› 정답 12쪽

1   Which words for the blanks are correct? (2 answers) 2점

> • Fred has _____ Japanese comic books.
> • How _____ did you pay for that cap?

① many – many   ② many – much   ③ much – many

④ lots of – much   ⑤ a lot of – many

2   다음 중 어법상 <u>어색한</u> 문장을 <u>모두</u> 고르시오. 2점

① Do you have any potatoes?

② The shop has plenty of big shoes.

③ I would like cold something now.

④ The restaurant is on the five floor, sir.

⑤ We all had many opinions about the matter.

3   우리말을 조건에 맞게 영작하시오. 3점

> 내 사촌은 절대 조금의 돈도 쓰지 않는다.
> ┈┈┈┈┈┈┈┈┈┈┈┈┈┈┈┈┈┈┈┈┈┈
> ·조건 1   never를 사용할 것
> ·조건 2   some 또는 any를 쓸 것
> ·조건 3   6단어로 쓸 것

→ _____

4   그림을 묘사하는 문장에서 어법상 <u>어색한</u> 부분을 <u>2개</u> 찾아 고쳐 쓰시오. 3점

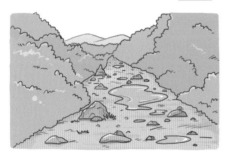

The river has few water and lot of stones.

_____ → _____

_____ → _____

VOCA   comic book 만화책 | pay 지불하다 | opinion 의견 | matter 문제

UNIT 19 부사

CONCEPT 1 부사의 역할과 형태

부사는 동사, 형용사, 다른 부사(구), 문장 전체를 꾸며주는 말이다.

She doesn't <u>cook</u> well. (동사 수식)　　She was a very <u>clever</u> girl. (형용사 수식)

Thank you very <u>much</u>. (부사 수식)　　Luckily, <u>they had enough time</u>. (문장 수식)

대부분의 형용사	+ -ly	kind → kindly, slow → slowly
'자음+y'로 끝나는 경우	y → i + -ly	easy → easily, happy → happily

CONCEPT 2 주의해야 할 부사

A 형용사와 형태가 같은 부사

- fast(빠른/빨리)　　　• early(이른/일찍)　　　• late(늦은/늦게)
- pretty(예쁜/꽤)　　　• hard(힘든, 딱딱한/열심히)

He is a fast runner. (형용사)　　She runs very fast. (부사)

B -ly를 붙여 뜻이 달라지는 부사

- late(늦은/늦게) – lately(최근에)　　• hard(열심히) – hardly(거의 ~ 않는)
- near(가까이) – nearly(거의)　　　• high(높은/높게) – highly(매우)

Lately, the show is popular.　　She hardly walks.

He nearly died in the war.　　I highly appreciate it.

C too와 either

'~도 역시'라는 뜻으로 too는 긍정문에, either는 부정문에 쓴다.

D well

well이 부사이면 '잘'이란 뜻이고, 형용사이면 '건강한'이란 뜻이다.

You did the job very well. (부사)　　She's not very well today. (형용사)

CONCEPT 3 빈도부사

빈도나 횟수를 나타내는 부사를 빈도부사라고 한다.

always	usually	often	sometimes	seldom	never
항상	대개, 보통	자주, 흔히	가끔, 때때로	좀처럼 ~ 않는	결코 ~ 아닌

The girl is never late.　　He seldom keeps his promises.

We sometimes play ping-pong.　　He often goes to the theater.

They don't usually walk to school.　　He is always polite at school.

GRAMMAR POINT

-ly로 끝나는 형용사

- 명사에 -ly가 붙어 형용사가 된 단어들을 부사로 혼동하지 않도록 주의해야 한다.

  manly(남자다운)

  friendly(상냥한)

  lovely(사랑스러운)

  daily(매일의)

  weekly(매주의)

  monthly(매달의)

  yearly(매년의)

neither

- 'not+either'를 neither로 쓴다.

  I didn't like the movie.

  – Me neither. (= I didn't like the movie either.)

too의 위치

- too가 '너무'의 뜻일 때는 형용사나 부사 앞에 온다.

  She is <u>too</u> generous.

빈도부사의 위치

- 빈도부사는 조동사나 be동사 뒤 또는 일반동사 앞에 위치한다.

  It <u>seldom</u> snows in Busan. (일반동사 앞)

  He is <u>often</u> late for school. (be동사 뒤)

- 의문문에서 빈도부사는 주어 뒤에 온다.

  Do you <u>usually</u> walk to school?

  Why is she <u>always</u> sad?

- sometimes는 문장의 앞 또는 뒤에도 올 수 있다.

  <u>Sometimes</u> she calls me early in the morning.

VOCA　appreciate 고마워하다 | keep one's promise 약속을 지키다 | ping-pong 탁구 | theater 극장 | polite 예의 바른 | generous 너그러운, 관대한

Let's Check It Out

A   [ ]에서 알맞은 것을 고르시오. 각 1점

1   She is a [quick / quickly] learner.
2   He [slow / slowly] walked into the room.
3   She [careful / carefully] cut the paper.
4   My daughter wasn't very [happy / happily].
5   I [real / really] enjoyed the dinner.

B   밑줄 친 단어가 [보기]에서와 쓰임이 같으면 =로, 아니면 ≠로 표시하시오. 각 1점

> 보기   The sailing ship arrived safely.

1   I was late for school.   → _____
2   My father drives too fast.   → _____
3   The shoe shop opens early.   → _____
4   Your son's fever is a bit high.   → _____
5   That guy is pretty cool.   → _____

C   우리말과 일치하도록 빈칸에 알맞은 말을 쓰시오. 각 1점

1   나는 독일어를 잘 못해.
    → I can't speak German very _____.

2   그녀도 나를 싫어한다.
    → She hates me, _____.

3   그들은 매우 열심히 일한다.
    → They work very _____.

4   최근에 그는 인도에서 돌아왔다.
    → _____, he returned from India.

D   괄호 안의 단어가 들어갈 수 있는 위치에 모두 V표 하시오. 각 1점

1   She talks to her ex-boyfriend. (never)
2   The twins are late for class. (often)
3   My mom and I go shopping. (sometimes)
4   What do you eat for lunch? (usually)

VOCA   sailing ship 대형 범선 | fever 열 | a bit 조금 | guy 남자 | German 독일어 | return 돌아오다 | ex-boyfriend 전 남자친구 | twin 쌍둥이

Ready for Exams

>>> 정답 12쪽

My score is

Let's Check It Out _____ / 18점   0~20점 → Level 1 Test
Ready for Exams _____ / 12점 → 21~25점 → Level 2 Test
Total _____ / 30점   26~30점 → Level 3 Test

91

1 다음 중 형용사-부사의 관계가 <u>아닌</u> 것의 개수는? 2점

• true – truly	• gentle – gently	• full – fully
• easy – easily	• friend – friendly	• simple – simply

① 1개　　　　　② 2개　　　　　③ 3개

④ 4개　　　　　⑤ 5개

2 Which of the underlined words is <u>incorrect</u>? 2점

① The thief ran so <u>fast</u>.

② Carmen dances very <u>good</u>.

③ I'd like to join the game, <u>too</u>.

④ Think <u>carefully</u> about your answer.

⑤ The old couple walked together <u>happily</u>.

3 다음 중 어법상 <u>어색한</u> 문장은? 2점

① Kate, he never trusted you.

② My friends are always cheerful.

③ Jack sometimes laughs at me.

④ They are often late for meetings.

⑤ Do usually you have dinner at home?

4 Rearrange the words to make a question. 3점

do, do, school, you, what, after, usually

→ _____

5 주어진 단어 중 필요한 **3단어**를 골라 그림에 맞는 문장을 완성하시오. 3점

balloon, balloons, flies, flew, high, highly

→ The _____ _____ _____ in the sky.

VOCA　thief 도둑 | join ~에 참여하다 | carefully 신중하게 | couple 부부 | trust 신뢰하다 | cheerful 명랑한 | laugh at 비웃다 | balloon 열기구

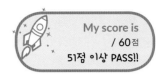
>>> 정답 13쪽

01 다음 중 밑줄 친 부분의 쓰임이 다른 하나는? 2점

① He has a <u>great</u> voice.
② We had a <u>great</u> weekend.
③ This is a <u>great</u> painting.
④ That was a <u>great</u> concert.
⑤ The movie is really <u>great</u>.

02 빈칸에 들어갈 수 <u>없는</u> 것은? 2점

> Mom, please buy _____ grapes.

① a lot of　　　　② lots of
③ much　　　　④ many
⑤ plenty of

03 다음 중 어법상 <u>어색한</u> 것으로 묶인 것은? 3점

 고난도

> ⓐ I am always happy.
> ⓑ Do usually you get up at five?
> ⓒ Mr. Kim is never late for work.
> ⓓ I walk often to school.
> ⓔ Sometimes you upset me.
> ⓕ I often dream about going to the stars.

① ⓐ, ⓑ　　　　② ⓑ, ⓓ
③ ⓑ, ⓓ, ⓔ　　　④ ⓑ, ⓒ, ⓔ
⑤ ⓑ, ⓔ, ⓕ

04 Which correction is right? (2 answers) 2점

 함정

> A: How many children do you have?
> B: I have seventh daughters. How about you?
> A: I don't have some children.

① How many → How much
② seventh → seven
③ daughters → daughter
④ some → any
⑤ some → much

05 괄호 안의 단어를 바르게 배열한 것은? 2점

 한눈에 쏙

> Thomas wanted to do (good, something, for, others).

① something others for good
② good something for others
③ good for others something
④ something good for others
⑤ for others good something

06 각 빈칸에 들어갈 말이 바르게 짝지어진 것은? 2점

> • Amy jumped into the water, and the other girls jumped, _____.
> • We didn't bring our bathing suits. We didn't bring our beach towels _____.

① too – too　　　　② too – either
③ too – neither　　④ either – either
⑤ either – neither

07 Which of the underlined words is correct?

 함정 (2 answers) 2점

① The dragonfly is flying <u>highly</u>.
② <u>Nearly</u> ten people were absent.
③ The new officer <u>hard</u> slept last night.
④ The plastic bottle was <u>near</u> empty.
⑤ We arrived thirty minutes <u>late</u>.

08 대화의 빈칸에 알맞은 말이 바르게 짝지어진 것은? 2점

> A: Are you ready to order?
> B: Yes. I want _____ cherry juice.
> A: Oh, we don't have _____ right now.

① any – any　　　　② any – some
③ some – any　　　④ some – some
⑤ some – another

09 ^{U19_3+GP}

다음 문장의 알맞은 곳에 'usually'를 추가하여 문장을
다시 쓰시오. 4점

> Wolves don't attack people.

→ _____

10 ^{U19_2A}

★ 고난도 조건에 맞게 우리말을 영작하시오. 7점

> 나는 꽤 피곤했다.
>
> ・어휘   be, tired
> ・조건   위의 단어 외에 아래 영영풀이가 설명하는 단어를 추
>   가할 것
>   We can use "p_____" as an adverb
>   before an adjective or another adverb. It
>   means "quite."
>   *adverb: 부사 **adjective: 형용사

→ _____

11 ^{U18_2+U19_GP}

주어진 단어들을 배열하여 우리말을 영작하시오. 4점

> 너무 많은 자존심은 너에게 좋지 않아.
>
> much, good, is, you, too, pride, not, for

→ _____

12 ^{U18_2}

In the dialog, find the error and correct it. 4점

> A: I can't wait for this Friday.
> B: Why? Do you have some special plans?
> A: My friends and I are going camping.
> B: That sounds exciting.

_____ → _____

13 ^{U19_2B}

👁 한눈에 쏙 각 빈칸에 공통으로 들어갈 단어를 쓰고, 그 단어가 문
장에서 하는 역할이 다른 것을 고르시오. 4점

> ⓐ It is a very _____ choice.
> ⓑ Everybody worked _____.
> ⓒ The bread is too _____.

→ _____, ( )

14 ^{U18_2}

조건에 맞도록 우리말을 영작하시오. 6점

> 그 마법사는 많은 구슬을 갖고 있었다.
>
> ・조건 l   p로 시작하는 단어를 반드시 쓸 것
> ・조건 2   어휘 – wizard, marble, have

→ _____

15 ^{U18_3}

다음 영작에서 어법상 <u>어색한</u> 부분을 찾아 고치시오. 4점

> 지금은 21세기이다.
> = It is the twenty-one century now.

_____ → _____

16 ^{U19_1}

Fill in the blank to make the two sentences
have the same meaning. 4점

> The principal is a very humorous speaker.

→ The principal speaks very _____.

17 ^{U19_2C}

그림을 보고, 조건에 맞게 (A)에 들어갈 말을 쓰시오. 6점

> W: I'm sorry. You're not my type.
> M: Don't be sorry. You're ___(A)___.
>
> ・조건 l   '역시'란 말을 문장 끝에 쓸 것
> ・조건 2   여자가 사용한 말을 이용할 것

(A) _____

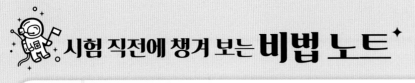
>>> 정답 13쪽

한눈에 쏙! 아래 노트를 보면서 빈칸을 채워 보세요.

1 수식 위치

-one, 1)-_ _ _ _ , 2)-_ _ _ _ _   →   형용사

2 기수와 서수

one – first   two – 1)_____   three – 2)_____

five – 3)_____   nine – 4)_____   twelve – 5)_____

3 부사

fast(빠른; 1)_____)   hard(딱딱한, 힘든; 2)_____)   3)_____(늦은; 늦게)   4)_____(최근에)

near(5)_____; _____)   nearly(6)_____)   7)_____(높은; 높게)   highly(8)_____)

4 빈도부사

1)a   →   2)u   →   3)o   →   4)s   →   5)s   →   6)n

*위치: 조동사/be동사 뒤, 일반동사 앞 ⨯ 의문문인 경우: 주어 뒤!

헷갈리지 말자! 초록색으로 표시된 부분을 바르게 고쳐 쓰세요.

1 We just met strange someone on the nineth floor.

2 They left lately on Friday afternoon.

3 Why is always everybody mad at me?

CHAPTER 07
비교 구문

UNIT 20 비교 변화, 동등 비교

CONCEPT 1 비교 변화

A 규칙 변화

대부분	+-er/-est	tall – taller – tallest small – smaller – smallest
-e로 끝나는 경우	+-r/-st	large – larger – largest nice – nicer – nicest
'자음+y'로 끝나는 경우	y → i+-er/-est	busy – busier – busiest happy – happier – happiest
'단모음+단자음'으로 끝나는 경우	마지막 자음+-er/-est	hot – hotter – hottest fat – fatter – fattest
대부분의 2음절, 3음절 이상	more/most+원급	famous – more famous – most famous important – more important – most important

B 불규칙 변화

- good/well – better – best
- many/much – more – most
- late(시간이 늦은) – later – latest
- bad/ill – worse – worst
- little – less – least
- late(순서가 늦은) – latter – last

CONCEPT 2 동등 비교

A 기본 형태

형태	의미
as+원급+as …	…만큼 ~한[-히, -게]

Your son is as tall as you now.

Your daughter smiles as happily as you.

He has as many pets as you do.

B 원급의 부정

형태	의미
not ~ as[so]+원급+as …	…만큼 ~하지 않은[않게]

Johnny is not as polite as you.

→ You are more polite than Johnny.

GRAMMAR POINT

more와 most를 붙이는 단어

- -ful, -ive, -ous, -ed, -ing, -ish, -ly로 끝나는 단어는 more와 most를 붙인다.

  tired – more tired – most tired

  useful – more useful – most useful

비교 대상 일치

- 동등 비교에서 비교 대상은 같은 것이어야 한다.

  My computer is as noisy as Mr. Lian. (→ Mr. Lian's)

「as + 형용사/부사 + as」 찾는 법

- as ~ as…를 없애면 된다.

  He lives as [simple / simply] as my grandmother.

  → He lives simply.

원급의 부정

- 일반 문장과 똑같이 부정한다.

  Your coffee is not as bad as mine.

  (be동사의 부정)

  They don't like me as much as my sister.

  (일반동사의 부정)

VOCA polite 예의 바른 | useful 유용한 | noisy 시끄러운

★ Let's Check It Out

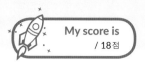
A 단어의 비교급과 최상급을 쓰시오. 각 1점

1 hot – _____ – _____

2 good – _____ – _____

3 smart – _____ – _____

4 large – _____ – _____

5 funny – _____ – _____

6 exciting – _____ – _____

7 quickly – _____ – _____

B [ ]에서 알맞은 것을 고르시오. 각 1점

1 I am as tall [so / as] my sister.

2 He is [as not / not as] cool as you.

3 Their house is as large as [us / ours].

4 She has as [much / many] friends as you.

C 괄호 안의 단어를 빈칸에 맞게 배열하시오. 각 1점

1 Hani runs _____. (Aeri, fast, as, as)

2 His sister watches _____. (you, much, as, as, TV)

3 She knows _____. (as, words, I, many, as)

D 우리말과 같은 뜻이 되도록 빈칸을 채우시오. 각 1점

1 나는 진우만큼 힘이 세다.

→ I am _____ strong _____ Jinwoo.

2 Gloria는 Luna만큼 재미있지 않다. (funny)

→ Gloria is _____ _____ _____ _____ Luna.

3 너의 피부는 우유만큼 하얗다.

→ Your skin is _____ _____ _____ _____.

4 그녀는 나만큼 신중하게 그것에 대해 생각했다. (carefully)

→ She thought about it _____ _____ _____

_____ did.

VOCA   carefully 신중하게

1   다음 중 원급-비교급-최상급의 관계가 <u>잘못된</u> 것의 개수는? 2점

- good – gooder – goodest
- big – bigger – biggest
- easy – easier – easiest
- helpful – helpfuler – helpfulest
- dangerous – more dangerous – most dangerous

① 1개   ② 2개   ③ 3개
④ 4개   ⑤ 5개

2   Which is NOT suitable for the blank? 3점

Lisa is as _____ as my sister.

① lovely   ② cute   ③ bravely
④ small   ⑤ smart

3   다음 중 어법상 어색한 것을 <u>모두</u> 고르시오. 3점

① I am as busy as Martin.
② He is as not honest as you.
③ She spoke as slowly as your teacher.
④ They collected as much shells as us.
⑤ Your sports car isn't as fast as my uncle.

4   괄호 안의 단어를 이용하여 그림에 맞는 문장을 완성하시오. 4점

→ The building on the left is _____ _____

_____ the one on the right. (high)

VOCA   helpful 도움이 되는 | collect 모으다, 수집하다 | shell 조개 껍데기

UNIT 21 비교급

1 비교급의 의미와 기본 형태

비교급을 이용하여 두 대상을 비교하는 것을 말한다.

형태	의미
-er than … 또는 more ~ than …	…보다 더 ~한[-히, -게]

A bee is smaller than a dragonfly.

She was more tired than her husband.

The store has more shoes than this store.

2 비교급의 부정과 열등 비교

형태	의미
not ~+비교급+than … less+원급+than … (열등 비교)	…보다 덜 ~한[-히, -게]

Today isn't colder than yesterday.

→Today is less cold than yesterday.

She doesn't have more money than you.

→ She has less money than you.

3 비교급 강조 부사

비교급을 강조하는 표현은 다음과 같으며, '훨씬'이라는 의미이다.

> much[still, even, far, a lot]+비교급+than ~

That bracelet is much prettier than this one.

Today, it rained a lot more than yesterday.

VOCA dragonfly 잠자리 | bracelet 팔찌 | item 품목 | circle 원

Let's Check It Out

>>> 정답 13쪽

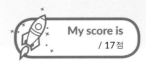

My score is
/ 17점

A   [ ]에서 알맞은 것을 고르시오. ^{각 1점}

1   Nancy is [busy / busier] than Nick.

2   He has [more / much] free time than her.

3   My sister isn't [diligenter / more diligent] than I.

4   Today is less [cold / colder] than yesterday.

5   This subject is [very / much] easier than that one.

B   괄호 안의 단어를 빈칸에 알맞은 형태로 쓰시오. ^{각 1점}

1   My hands aren't _____ than yours. (big)

2   The play was _____ _____ than the movie. (interesting)

3   My new roommate eats _____ than me. (little)

4   He is _____ at running than my sister. (bad)

5   Are women _____ _____ than men? (careful)

C   밑줄 친 부분을 바르게 고쳐 쓰시오. ^{각 1점}

1   Baseball is <u>popular</u> than soccer.   → _____

2   A dog runs less <u>faster</u> than a horse.   → _____

3   Harry studies <u>very</u> harder than John.   → _____

D   우리말과 같은 뜻이 되도록 빈칸을 채우시오. ^{각 1점}

1   너의 컴퓨터는 내 것보다 느리구나.

→ Your computer is _____ _____ mine.

2   너에겐 수학이 영어보다 더 흥미롭니?

→ Is math _____ _____ _____ English to you?

3   그가 너보다 훨씬 더 일찍 왔어.

→ He came here _____ earlier than you.

4   한국에선 J-pop이 K-pop보다 덜 인기 있어.

→ J-pop is _____ _____ _____ K-pop in Korea.

VOCA   subject 과목 | play 연극 | roommate 룸메이트 | careful 조심스러운 | J-pop 일본 가요

1 Which is proper for the blank? 2점

> A: Seron, how do you feel today?
> B: Doctor, I feel _____ than yesterday.

① good   ② best   ③ better
④ well   ⑤ happy

2 두 문장의 뜻이 같도록 할 때 빈칸에 알맞은 것은? 3점

> I am not as busy as Morris.
> = Morris is _____ I.

① as busy as   ② busier than   ③ not as busy as
④ less busy than   ⑤ not busier than

3 어법상 어색한 것을 찾아 바르게 고쳐 쓴 학생은? 3점

> My little sister's desk is very cleaner than mine.

① 민준: little → less
② 현우: sister's → sisters
③ 예준: very → much
④ 상우: mine → my
⑤ 우진: cleaner → more clean

4 그림을 보고 조건에 맞게 문장을 완성하시오. 5점

· 조건 1 비교 구문을 사용할 것
· 조건 2 키에 관한 것만 쓸 것
· 조건 3 부정문을 사용하지 말 것

→ Ava is _____ _____ Laura, but she is

_____ _____ Ted.

UNIT
22 최상급

1 최상급의 의미와 기본 형태

최상급을 이용하여 둘 이상의 대상을 비교하는 것을 말한다.

형태	의미
the -est 또는 most ~	가장 ~한[-히, -게]

That was the worst choice of her life.

This is the largest room in this hotel, sir.

It was the most interesting drawing of all.

2 최상급과 전치사

최상급 뒤에 오는 말에 따라 전치사가 달라진다.

형태	의미
최상급+of+복수 명사(비교 대상)	… 중에서 가장 ~한[-히,-게]
최상급+in+단수 명사(장소, 집단)	…에서 가장 ~한[-히,-게]

What is the fastest of all animals?

Taylor plays basketball the best in town.

3 one of the + 최상급 + 복수 명사

형태	의미
one of the+최상급+복수 명사	가장 ~한 … 중 하나

Andrew is one of the best b-boys in Canada.

The actress drives one of the most expensive cars in Korea.

GRAMMAR POINT

'최상급 + 명사'에서 명사의 생략

- 명사를 짐작할 수 있을 때 '최상급+명사'에서 명사가 생략될 수 있다.

  Grace is the oldest (child) in her family.

the를 생략해도 되는 경우

- 부사의 최상급에서는 the를 생략할 수 있다.

  He always works (the) hardest in the office.

- 형용사가 홀로 서술적 용법으로 사용될 때 the를 생략할 수 있다.

  What is the hottest month in Korea?

  – August is (the) hottest.

VOCA choice 선택 | drawing 그림 | b-boy 비보이(힙합[랩] 음악을 하는 사람 또는 팬) | actress 여배우 | expensive 비싼

A [ ]에서 알맞은 것을 고르시오. 각 1점

1 Julie is [tallest / the tallest] in her family.

2 Mount Everest is the world's [higher / highest] mountain.

3 Summer is the hottest [in / of] the four seasons.

4 Bobsleigh is one of the most exciting [sports / sport].

B 괄호 안의 단어를 빈칸에 알맞은 형태로 쓰시오. 각 1점

1 My backpack was the _____ of them all. (heavy)

2 Ted is the _____ in my family. (young)

3 Mark is the _____ _____ student in my class. (diligent)

4 He is the _____ _____ man of the five. (important)

5 Harris came in _____ of all the players. (late)

C 밑줄 친 부분을 바르게 고치시오. 각 1점

1 It's <u>oldest</u> tree in this town.　　→ _____

2 It was the <u>boringest</u> movie of all.　　→ _____

3 The strings are <u>the larger</u> group in the orchestra.　　→ _____

4 This car is the <u>most fastest</u> of them all.　　→ _____

5 Jeju-do is one of the most beautiful <u>island</u> in the world.　　→ _____

D 괄호 안의 단어를 활용하여 우리말과 일치하도록 문장을 완성하시오. 각 1점

1 당신은 여기서 최고의 피자를 먹을 수 있습니다. (good)

→ You can enjoy _____ _____ pizza here.

2 그가 우리 반에서 가장 인기 있는 학생이야. (popular)

→ He is _____ _____ _____ student in my class.

3 장미가 모든 꽃 중에서 제일 예뻐. (pretty)

→ The rose is _____ _____ _____ all flowers.

VOCA　season 계절 | bobsleigh 봅슬레이 | backpack 배낭 | diligent 부지런한 | the strings 현악 파트 | orchestra 오케스트라, 관현악단 | island 섬

Ready for Exams

>>> 정답 14쪽

My score is

Let's Check It Out _____ / 17점   0~20점 → Level 1 Test
Ready for Exams _____ / 13점   ➡   21~25점 → Level 2 Test
Total _____ / 30점   26~30점 → Level 3 Test

1 빈칸에 가장 적절한 것은? 2점

> Gyuro is the _____ student in the soccer club.

① young   ② younger   ③ youngest

④ older   ⑤ less old

2 Which is true according to the picture? (Find ALL.) 3점

Highest Ranked Games		
Rank	Application	Price
1	Mr. Giggle	$2.99
2	Shape Shift	FREE
3	Army of Darkness	$4.99

① Shape Shift is the cheapest of all.

② Mr. Giggle is less popular than Shape Shift.

③ Army of Darkness is the most expensive of the three.

④ Shape Shift is not as popular as Mr. Giggle.

⑤ Mr. Giggle's ranking is the highest of all.

3 다음 중 어법상 어색한 문장을 모두 고르시오. 3점

① Dasom is the fastest swimmer of all my classmates.

② Bakken in Denmark is the oldest amusement park in the world.

③ He was the most quickest of all the staff.

④ The African grey parrot is one of the smartest animal.

⑤ Math is the hardest of all subjects.

4 주어진 단어를 활용하여 우리말을 영작하시오. 5점

> 프라이드치킨이 세상에서 가장 맛있는 음식이다. (delicious, fried chicken)

→ _____

VOCA ranking 순위 | amusement park 놀이공원 | staff (모든) 직원 | parrot 앵무새 | fried chicken 프라이드치킨

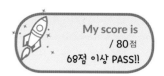

>>> 정답 14쪽

01 U20_1A+1B+GP

다음 중 원급-비교급-최상급의 관계가 <u>잘못된</u> 것끼리 묶인 것은? 2점

ⓐ well – better – best
ⓑ tall – taller – tallest
ⓒ bad – worse – worst
ⓓ sunny – sunnyer – sunnyest
ⓔ pretty – more pretty – most pretty
ⓕ foolish – foolisher – foolishest

① ⓐ, ⓒ, ⓓ　　② ⓐ, ⓓ, ⓔ　　③ ⓑ, ⓓ, ⓔ
④ ⓒ, ⓔ, ⓕ　　⑤ ⓓ, ⓔ, ⓕ

02 U20_2

Which describes the picture correctly?
(2 answers) 2점

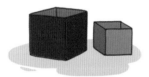

① The red box is as small as the blue one.
② The red box is not as big as the blue one.
③ The blue box is not as big as the red one.
④ The blue box is as big as the red one.
⑤ The red box isn't as small as the blue one.

03 U20_2+U21_2

우리말을 영어로 바르게 옮긴 학생은? (답 2개) 2점

한국에서 축구는 야구만큼 인기가 있지 않다.

① 민기: In Korea, soccer is as popular as baseball.
② 기리: In Korea, soccer is not so popular as baseball.
③ 예준: Soccer is less popular than baseball in Korea.
④ 건우: Soccer is more popular than baseball in Korea.
⑤ 우진: Soccer is the most popular sport of all in Korea.

04 U21_1+3

다음을 영작할 때 필요 <u>없는</u> 단어 2개는? 2점

내 성적은 전보다 훨씬 더 나쁘다.

① grades　　　　② much
③ very　　　　　④ worse
⑤ as

05 U21_1

다음은 윤하네 반 학생들이 좋아하는 과목을 나타낸 그래프이다. 그래프를 올바르게 설명한 것은? (답 2개) 2점

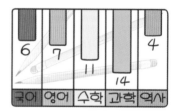

① The students like Korean more than math.
② The students like English more than math.
③ The students like science more than Korean.
④ The students like history more than math.
⑤ The students like science more than English.

06 U22_2

각 빈칸에 들어갈 말이 바르게 짝지어진 것은? 2점

• Jenny is _____ girl in our town.
• The cherry tomato is _____ vegetable in this garden.

① clever – small
② cleverer – smaller
③ cleverest – smallest
④ the cleverer – the smaller
⑤ the cleverest – the smallest

07 다음 문장에서 오류를 찾아 바르게 고친 학생은? 2점

> I think he's the world's most strongest man.

① 승화: the world's → world's
② 지민: most → best
③ 가빈: most → 삭제
④ 은빛: man → men
⑤ 은조: strongest → strong

08 다음 중 어법상 <u>어색한</u> 문장의 개수는? 2점

★고난도

> ⓐ This cookie is as delicious as that one.
> ⓑ He's one of the laziest boy in the class.
> ⓒ It's much more colder than yesterday.
> ⓓ Son Heung-min is the most soccer player in Korea.

① 1개 ② 2개
③ 3개 ④ 4개
⑤ 어색한 문장 없음

09 주어진 문장과 의미가 같은 것은? 2점

> Lily is not as talkative as her little sister.

① Lily is as talkative as her little sister.
② Lily is more talkative than her little sister.
③ Lily's little sister is as talkative as Lily.
④ Lily's little sister is not as talkative as Lily.
⑤ Lily's little sister is more talkative than Lily.

10 Among the underlined, which is wrong? 2점

① Minsik is <u>the worst guy</u> in his town.
② <u>The biggest city</u> in Korea isn't Incheon.
③ He was <u>the fattest</u> of the four.
④ What's <u>the most beautiful beach</u> in Korea?
⑤ Hamburgers are <u>the most tasty food</u> to me.

11 다음 두 문장을 한 문장으로 바르게 전환한 것은? 2점

> Judy has a 40-inch monitor. Nana also has a 40-inch monitor.

① Judy's monitor isn't as big as Nana's.
② Judy's monitor is as big as Nana's.
③ Judy's monitor is bigger than Nana's.
④ Nana's monitor isn't as big as Judy's.
⑤ Nana's monitor is less big than Judy's.

12 다음 문장에서 어법상 <u>어색한</u> 것을 찾아 바르게 고친 것은? 2점

함정

> Nobody was less sillier than Ondal.

① was → were   ② less → more
③ sillier → silly   ④ than → as
⑤ Ondal → Ondal's

13 주어진 단어들을 조합하여 어법상 옳은 문장을 만들 수 있는 것은? 4점

★고난도

① He / faster / . / me / runs / than / most
② math / interestingest / ? / subject / the / Is
③ director / . / is / the / Mr. Bong / movie / greatest
④ Did / arrive / they / ? / us / than / more / earlier
⑤ / today / will / . / hotter / the / be / Tomorrow / than

14 다음 중 어법상 옳은 것은? (정답 최대 3개) 3점

★고난도

① Your grade is best than mine.
② Harry is as diligently as Chloe.
③ Earth is largest than the moon.
④ Paju is much more peaceful than Pyeongyang.
⑤ Rocky is one of the most hardworking boys in class.

15 Choose the <u>necessary</u> words and rearrange them. 4점

U20_2

함정

> Messi, as, as, than, good, well, soccer, play

→ I _____ .

16 두 문장 중 어법상 <u>어색한</u> 것을 찾아 바르게 고치시오. 4점

U21_1

> ⓐ He passed the ball as smoothly as I.
> ⓑ She has much little experience than me.

(   ) _____ → _____

17 두 문장의 의미가 같도록 빈칸에 알맞은 말을 쓰시오. 4점

U20_2

> This house is 100 years old. That tree is also 100 years old.

→ That house is _____ _____ _____ that tree.

18 다음 문장을 기초로 조건에 맞게 영작하시오. 각 4점

U21_1+U20_2B

> I'm fourteen years old, and my brother is nineteen years old.
>
> ·조건1   (1)은 비교급을 쓸 것
> ·조건2   (2)는 원급을 쓸 것

(1) My brother is _____ _____ me.

(2) I am _____ _____ _____ _____ my brother.

19 [보기]를 참고하여 우리말을 영어로 옮기시오. 6점

U20_1A+U22_2

> 보기   Jaykeun is a popular student.
>
> 재근이는 우리 반에서 가장 인기 있는 학생이다.

→ _____

20 Look at the picture and answer each question with a complete sentence. 각 4점

U21_1+U22_1

> Q: Which is bigger than the others?
> A: (1) _____
> Q: Which is the oldest of the three?
> A: (2) _____

21 어법상 어색한 문장들의 첫 글자를 빈칸에 쓰시오. 6점

U20_1A+U22_1

고난도

> ⓐ He could jump as high as I could.
> ⓑ Greg is not more older than his girlfriend.
> ⓒ Tennis is less popular than badminton.
> ⓓ No, she's not the most funniest girl.
> ⓔ He's one of the nicest students in town.
> ⓕ UFO is the most mysterious band names.

→ You are a ☐e☐i☐s!

22 Fill in the blanks according to the table. (Use the words "light," "heavy," or "tall.") 각 3점

U20_2+U21_2+U22_2

한눈에 쏙

	Cindy	Buffy	Jenny
Weight	49kg	52kg	52kg
Height	168cm	172cm	164cm

(1) Buffy is as _____ as Jenny.

(2) Jenny is less _____ than Buffy.

(3) Cindy is the _____ of the three.

한눈에 쏙! 아래 노트를 보면서 빈칸을 채워 보세요.

1 비교 변화

busy – 1)_____ – 2)_____

fat – 3)_____ – 4)_____

important – 5)_____ – 6)_____

good/7)_____ – 8)_____ – 9)_____

10)_____/11)_____ – worse – 12)_____

2 동등 비교

as + 1)_____(형용사/부사) + as

3 비교급

-er/more ~ + 1)

☆ 강조 부사: much, 2)s_____, 3)e_____, 4)f_____, a lot

4 최상급

the + -est /most ~ +
- 1)_____+복수 명사(비교 대상)
- in+장소, 2)_____

헷갈리지 말자! 초록색으로 표시된 부분을 바르게 고쳐 쓰세요.

1 Those shoes are not as comfortably as these.
   ⌐→

2 Your bike is much more big than mine.
   ⌐→

3 Michelle is one of the happiest girl in the world.
   ⌐→

CHAPTER 08
to부정사

명사적 용법

CONCEPT 1 to부정사

to부정사는 'to + 동사원형'의 형태로 문장에서 동사가 아니라 명사, 형용사, 부사의 역할을 한다.

	to부정사	전치사
뒤에 오는 것	to + 동사원형	to + 명사/동명사
해석	~하는 것, ~하는, ~하기 위해 등	~로, ~에게
예문	He likes to sing.	He went to the park.

CONCEPT 2 to부정사의 명사적 용법

to부정사가 문장 안에서 명사처럼 사용되는 경우를 'to부정사의 명사적 용법'이라고 한다. '~하기, ~하는 것'이라는 의미이며, 문장 안에서 주어, 보어, 목적어의 역할을 한다.

문장 성분	위치	예문
주어(~하는 것은)	문장 앞	To learn a foreign language is hard. = It is hard to learn a foreign language.
보어(~하는 것이다)	be동사, seem 뒤	My dream is to be a model.
목적어(~하는 것을)	일반동사 뒤	I want to be a lawyer.

CONCEPT 3 의문사 + to부정사

'의문사 + to부정사'는 「의문사 + 주어 + should + 동사원형」으로 풀어 쓸 수 있다.

형태	의미	예문
what + to부정사	무엇을 ~할지	Let us know what to do. = Let us know what we should do.
who(m) + to부정사	누구를 ~할지	I decided who(m) to invite. = I decided who(m) I should invite.
how + to부정사	어떻게 ~할지, ~하는 방법	I know how to cook. = I know how I should cook.
when + to부정사	언제 ~할지	We decided when to start. = We decided when we should start.
where + to부정사	어디에서 ~할지	Do you know where to go? = Do you know where you should go?

가주어 it

• to부정사가 주어 자리에 올 때 가주어 it을 쓰고 to부정사를 문장 뒤로 보낼 수 있다.

  To play computer games is exciting.
  → It is exciting to play computer games.

to부정사만 목적어로 취하는 동사

• agree: 동의하다
• pretend: ~인 척 하다
• hope: 바라다
• want: 원하다
• wish: 바라다
• decide: 결정하다
• plan: 계획하다
• expect: 기대하다
• promise: 약속하다

의문사 + to부정사

• '의문사 + to부정사'도 명사적 용법으로 사용된다.

  What to do is important.
  (주어)

  The problem is what to do.
  (보어)

  I don't know what to do.
  (목적어)

VOCA foreign 외국의 | language 언어 | model 모델 | lawyer 변호사 | exciting 신나는, 재미있는

Let's Check It Out

>>> 정답 15쪽

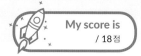

A [ ]에서 알맞은 것을 고르시오. 각 1점

1 He wants to [buy / buys] some fruit.

2 She went [to the store / the store].

3 [Teach / To teach] is to learn.

4 I sent flowers [to her / to she].

5 They came [to the wedding / to be the wedding].

B 밑줄 친 'to'가 부정사의 'to'이면 '부정사'라고 쓰고, 전치사 'to'이면 '전치사'라고 쓰시오.
각 1점

1 He gave three books <u>to</u> her.　　　　→ _____

2 My dream is <u>to</u> become a basketball player.　　→ _____

3 Harper started <u>to</u> run.　　　　　　→ _____

4 Judy and Julie went <u>to</u> bed.　　　　→ _____

C 밑줄 친 부분의 to부정사의 역할을 '주어', '보어', '목적어'로 구분하시오. 각 1점

1 I want <u>to have pizza</u>.　　　　　　　→ _____

2 His habit is <u>to ask questions repeatedly</u>.　→ _____

3 <u>To sing a song loudly</u> is fun for me.　　→ _____

4 He didn't know <u>what to do</u>.　　　　→ _____

5 It is important <u>to look ahead</u>.　　　→ _____

D 괄호 안의 단어들을 빈칸에 바르게 배열하시오. 각 1점

1 I hardly knew _____ to her.

   (to, what, say)

2 He doesn't know _____ the answer.

   (how, choose, to)

3 Will you tell me _____ ?

   (when, press, the button, to)

4 Did he learn _____ ?

   (how, to, swim)

VOCA wedding 결혼(식) | habit 습관 | ask 묻다 | repeatedly 반복적으로 | ahead 앞으로 | hardly 거의 ~ 않다 | choose 선택하다 | press 누르다

★ **Ready for Exams**

>>> 정답 15쪽

My score is

Let's Check It Out _____ / 18점   0~20점 → Level 1 Test
Ready for Exams _____ / 12점   21~25점 → Level 2 Test
Total _____ / 30점   26~30점 → Level 3 Test

1 다음 중 밑줄 친 'to'의 쓰임이 나머지와 다른 하나는? 2점

① He didn't go <u>to</u> college.
② <u>To</u> watch an action movie is exciting.
③ She continued <u>to</u> chat on KakaoTalk.
④ It's a pleasure <u>to</u> meet you.
⑤ She loves <u>to</u> play the piano.

2 Which is correct for the blank? 3점

My sister wanted _____ the orange dress.

① buy   ② to buy   ③ to bought
④ bought   ⑤ for buying

3 밑줄 친 부분의 쓰임이 [보기]와 같은 것은? 3점

She didn't want <u>to live</u> with a roommate.

① It is bad <u>to eat</u> a lot of food at night.
② <u>To jog</u> every day is good for your health.
③ My dream is <u>to be</u> a singer.
④ Is it really hard <u>to get</u> a perfect score?
⑤ Does he want <u>to be</u> a movie star?

4 그림을 보고 빈칸에 알맞은 말을 쓰시오. 4점

→ She doesn't know _____ _____ ride a bike.

VOCA   action movie 액션 영화 | college 대학 | continue 계속하다 | pleasure 기쁨 | jog 조깅하다 | perfect score 만점

112

UNIT 24 형용사적 용법, 부사적 용법

CONCEPT 1 to부정사의 형용사적 용법

to부정사가 문장 안에서 형용사처럼 사용되는 경우를 'to부정사의 형용사적 용법'이라고 부른다. '~할, ~하는'의 의미로 문장 안에서 명사나 대명사를 뒤에서 꾸며 주는 역할을 한다.

명사+to부정사	I have lots of things to do. (나는 할 일이 많다.)
대명사+to부정사	I want something to drink. (뭔가 마실 것이 필요해.)
명사+to부정사+전치사	He has no chair to sit on. (그는 앉을 의자가 없다.)
It's time+to부정사	It's time to leave. (떠날 시간이다.)

CONCEPT 2 to부정사의 부사적 용법

to부정사가 문장 안에서 부사처럼 사용되는 경우를 'to부정사의 부사적 용법'이라고 한다. '~하기 위해, ~해서, ~하다니, ~해서 (결국) …하다' 등으로 해석한다. to부정사가 부사처럼 동사, 형용사, 다른 부사를 수식한다.

목적(~하기 위해)	He ran around to keep warm. (그는 몸을 따뜻하게 유지하려고 이리 저리 뛰어다녔다.)
원인(~해서)	She was happy to meet him. (그녀는 그를 만나서 행복했다.)
형용사 수식(~하기에)	The question is hard to answer. (그 질문은 답하기에 어렵다.)
결과(~해서 …하다)	He lived to be 100 years old. (그는 살아서 100살이 되었다.)

CONCEPT 3 부사적 용법의 too ~ to...와 enough to...

| too+형용사/부사+to부정사
= so+형용사/부사+that+주어+can't ~ | 너무 ~해서 …할 수 없다 |
| 형용사/부사+enough+to부정사
= so+형용사/부사+that+주어+can ~ | …할 만큼 충분히 ~하다 |

I am too tired to work.

= I am so tired that I can't work. (나는 너무 피곤해서 일을 할 수 없다.)

We're close enough to share everything.

= We're so close that we can share everything. (우리는 모든 것을 공유할 만큼 가깝다.)

GRAMMAR POINT

-thing, -body, -one

- -thing, -body, -one으로 끝나는 대명사는 형용사가 뒤에서 꾸민다.
- 형용사와 to부정사가 대명사를 같이 수식할 경우에는 「대명사+형용사+to부정사」 순으로 한다.

  He needs something cold to drink.

  (그는 차가운 마실 것이 필요하다.)

명사 + to부정사 + 전치사

- to부정사의 꾸밈을 받는 명사가 전치사의 목적어인 경우, to부정사 뒤에 있는 전치사를 생략해서는 안 된다.

  We need some paper to write on.

  (우리는 위에 쓸 종이가 필요하다.)

  She doesn't have a pen to write with.

  (그녀는 가지고 쓸 펜이 없다.)

to부정사의 부정

- to부정사의 부정은 to부정사 바로 앞에 not이나 never를 붙인다.

  I decided not to use my cell phone after 10 p.m.

  (나는 오후 10시 이후에는 휴대전화를 사용하지 않기로 결심했다.)

시제 일치

- so ~ that... 구문에서 can은 주절의 동사 시제와 일치시킨다.

  I was too tired to work.

  = I was so tired that I couldn't work.

VOCA something 어떤 것 | run around 이리저리 뛰어다니다 | enough 충분한, 충분히 | share 공유하다

Let's Check It Out

>>> 정답 15쪽

A 밑줄 친 부분을 바르게 해석하시오. 각 1점

1 I don't have <u>anything to eat</u>.

→ 나는 _____이 아무것도 없다.

2 It's time <u>to watch</u> my favorite soap opera.

→ 내가 제일 좋아하는 드라마 _____ 시간이다.

3 The poor man didn't have <u>a house to live in</u>.

→ 그 가엾은 남자는 _____이 없었다.

B 괄호 안에 주어진 단어들을 빈칸에 바르게 배열하시오. 각 1점

1 그들은 마실 물이 없었다. (water, no, to, drink)

→ They had _____.

2 너는 쓸 연필이 필요하니? (to, a pencil, with, write)

→ Do you need _____?

C 밑줄 친 부분의 해석에 해당하는 것을 [보기]에서 고르시오. 각 1점

보기	(가) 목적(~하기 위해)	(나) 원인(~해서)	(다) 결과(~해서 …하다)

1 He was happy <u>to pass</u> the test.   → _____

2 I went to the river <u>to swim</u>.   → _____

3 He grew up <u>to be</u> a scientist.   → _____

D 빈칸에 알맞은 말을 써 넣으시오. 각 2점

1 You are too young to help me.

→ You are _____ young _____ you _____ help me.

2 He is smart enough to solve the problem.

→ He is _____ smart _____ he _____ solve the problem.

3 We are so tired that we can't walk.

→ We are _____ tired _____ _____.

VOCA soap opera 연속극, 드라마 | pass 통과하다 | scientist 과학자 | solve 풀다

My score is

Let's Check It Out _____ / 14점
Ready for Exams _____ / 11점
Total _____ / 25점

0~17점 → Level 1 Test
18~21점 → Level 2 Test
22~25점 → Level 3 Test

>>> 정답 15쪽

1 다음 두 문장에 대한 설명으로 <u>잘못된</u> 것은? (정답 2개) 3점

> ⓐ I am so happy to meet you.
> ⓑ They wanted to drink more water.

① ⓐ 형용사를 꾸미므로 형용사적 용법이다.

② ⓑ '마셔서'라고 해석한다.

③ ⓐ는 부사적 용법이다.

④ ⓑ는 명사처럼 사용되었다.

⑤ ⓐ와 ⓑ 둘 다 to부정사이다.

2 [보기]의 밑줄 친 부분과 쓰임이 같은 것은? 2점

> I went to California <u>to study</u> English.

① I want <u>to sing</u> some songs.

② Do you want something hot <u>to drink</u>?

③ She was surprised <u>to hear</u> my news.

④ I used the Internet <u>to do</u> my homework.

⑤ She grew up <u>to be</u> a fine police officer.

3 Which sentence is grammatically <u>incorrect</u>? 2점

① She studied hard to get a good score.

② Do you know where to get off?

③ She is not a person to lie.

④ Be careful to not catch a cold.

⑤ He needs a friend to talk with.

4 주어진 단어를 바르게 배열하여 우리말을 영작하시오. 4점

> 그녀는 그 이야기를 이해할 만큼 충분히 똑똑하다.
> she, smart, is, enough, to, the story, understand

→ _____

VOCA surprised 놀란 | fine 멋진, 훌륭한 | police officer 경찰관 | get off 내리다

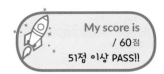
>>> 정답 16쪽

U23_1

01 밑줄 친 'to'의 쓰임이 같은 것끼리 묶인 것은? 2점

ⓐ I don't want <u>to</u> eat anything.

ⓑ Does she like <u>to</u> skate?

ⓒ Did you go <u>to</u> the department store?

ⓓ I'll show the picture <u>to</u> you.

ⓔ Are you going <u>to</u> San Francisco?

ⓕ Is it your job <u>to</u> teach English?

① ⓐ, ⓑ, ⓒ   ② ⓐ, ⓑ, ⓕ

③ ⓐ, ⓒ, ⓕ   ④ ⓒ, ⓔ, ⓕ

⑤ ⓓ, ⓔ, ⓕ

U23_2

02 Which is proper for the blank? 2점

They started _____ their assignment.

① did   ② do

③ to do   ④ to doing

⑤ for doing

U23_3

03 우리말과 같은 뜻이 되도록 할 때 빈칸에 알맞은 것은?

2점

그는 세탁기 사용하는 방법을 배웠다.

= He learned _____ the washing machine.

① how to use   ② where use to

③ what to use   ④ what use

⑤ how use

U24_GP

04 다음 중 어법상 어색한 문장은? 2점

① I decided to not watch TV.

② She planned to leave early.

③ We agreed to help him.

④ They came to meet her.

⑤ I was angry to lose the game.

[05~06] 밑줄 친 부분의 쓰임이 <u>다른</u> 하나를 고르시오. 각 2점

U23_2+U24_1

05 ① It's time <u>to dance</u>.

② We need a place <u>to live in</u>.

③ I want something <u>to chew</u>.

④ It's easy <u>to fix</u> the bike.

⑤ He forgot his promise <u>to meet</u> his friend.

U23_2+U24_1

06 ① I want <u>to work</u> with you.

② I love <u>to cook</u> Korean food.

③ We hope <u>to create</u> more jobs.

④ There are many things <u>to read</u>.

⑤ She planned <u>to travel</u> around the world.

U24_1

07 Which word is NOT needed when translating the sentence? 2점

이제 우리를 멈출 것은 없다.

① is   ② to

③ there   ④ nothing

⑤ stopping

U24_1+GP

08 다음 문장들을 바르게 설명한 학생은? 2점

ⓐ We have lots of paper to write.

ⓑ We need something cool to drink.

ⓒ Mary has nowhere to go.

① 윤희: ⓐ to write가 앞에 있는 paper를 꾸며주며 틀린 것이 없다.

② 미나: ⓑ something은 to drink 앞에 와야 한다.

③ 철수: ⓐ '위에 쓸 종이'이므로 전치사 on이 필요하다.

④ 진아: ⓒ to go는 nowhere 앞에 와야 한다.

⑤ 주혜: ⓑ something to drink cool의 순서가 맞다.

U23_2

09 Complete the sentence describing the picture. Use the given words. 4점

> eat, fried chicken

→ I want _____.

U23_GP

10 빈칸에 알맞은 단어를 쓰시오. 4점

> _____ is difficult to hide your feelings.

U23_GP

11 다음 그림을 보고 'it'과 'to'를 써서 8단어로 문장을 완성하시오. 4점

함정

> fun, play, the board game

→ _____

U24_2

12 to부정사를 사용해 두 문장을 한 문장으로 나타내시오. 5점

> I went to the Han River. I wanted to take a walk.

→ _____

U24_GP

13 다음 단어들을 나열해서 문장을 만드시오. 4점

> needs, he, hot, to, something, drink

→ _____

U23_3

14 Write the proper words for the blank so that the sentences have the same meaning. 4점

> She is asking where to find the truth.

→ She is asking _____

_____.

U24_2

15 두 문장의 의미가 같도록 빈칸에 알맞은 말을 쓰시오. 4점

> Yuna grew up and became a famous figure skater.

→ Yuna grew up _____ _____
 a famous figure skater.

U24_1+3

16 조건에 맞게 우리말을 영작하시오. 6점

한눈에 쏙

> 우리는 숙제가 너무 많아서 놀 시간이 없다.
>
> ·조건 1 to, much, too, play, time을 포함시킬 것
> ·조건 2 10단어로 쓸 것

→ _____

U24_3

17 주어진 단어를 어법에 맞게 배열하여 완전한 문장을 쓰시오. 5점

> to, color, enough, is, your hair, healthy

→ _____

U24_GP

18 다음 문장에서 어법상 어색한 부분을 찾아 바르게 고치시오. 4점

함정

> I was so ashamed that I can't raise my head.

_____ → _____

시험 직전에 챙겨 보는 비법 노트

한눈에 쏙! 아래 노트를 보면서 빈칸을 채워 보세요.

1 to부정사: 동사의 품사를 바꾸는 것

    to+1)_____

2 to부정사의 용법

① 명사적 용법	해석: 1)_____	동사 ➡ 명사
② 형용사적 용법	해석: ~하는	동사 ➡ 형용사
③ 2)_____ 용법	목적(3)_____), 원인(~해서), 형용사 수식(~하기에), 결과(~해서 …하다)	동사 ➡ 부사

3 too ~ to...와 enough to...

- ☆ 1)_____ ~ 2)_____ ...= so ~ that+주어+can't (너무 ~해서 …할 수 없다)
- 3)_____ to... = so ~ that+주어+can (…할 만큼 충분히 ~하다)

헷갈리지 말자! 초록색으로 표시된 부분을 바르게 고쳐 쓰세요.

1 I was too tired to work. = I was so tired that I <u>can't</u> work.

2 I decided <u>to not use</u> my cell phone too often.

3 We need two more chairs to <u>sit</u>.

4 The cave was <u>enough dark</u> to hide in.

CHAPTER 09
동명사

UNIT 25 동명사

GRAMMAR POINT

동명사 만들기
• 동명사 만드는 법은 p. 48 –ing 만드는 법 참조.

CONCEPT 1 동명사의 의미와 형태

동사를 명사처럼 사용하기 위해 동사 뒤에 -ing를 붙여 사용하는 것을 말한다.

형태	의미
동사원형+-ing	~하기, ~하는 것

동명사 주어
• 동명사 주어는 단수 취급한다.
Making accessories <u>is</u> a lot of fun.

동명사만 목적어로 취하는 동사
• enjoy: 즐기다
• mind: 꺼리다
• give up: 포기하다
• finish: 끝내다
• stop: 그만두다
• avoid: 피하다
• practice: 연습하다
• keep: 계속 ~하다

CONCEPT 2 동명사의 역할

문장 성분	위치	예문
주어	문장 앞	Sleeping well is important.
보어	be동사 뒤	His hobby is doing yoga.
목적어	동사 뒤	He enjoys swimming in the rain.
	전치사 뒤	Anita is good at speaking Korean.

동명사와 to부정사 둘 다 목적어로 취하는 동사
• like: 좋아하다
• love: 아주 좋아하다
• start, begin: 시작하다
• continue: 계속하다

CONCEPT 3 동명사와 현재분사

동명사	My hobby is collecting rocks. (내 취미는 돌을 수집하는 것이다.)
현재분사	I am collecting rocks now. (나는 지금 돌을 수집하고 있다.)

동명사 대신 명사를 써도 되는 경우
• '~을 먹고 싶다'
Man, I feel like some water now.
cf. I feel like an idiot.
(~처럼 느껴지다)
• '~을 고대하다'
I'm looking forward to your reply.
• on + 명사
They spend too much money on their house.

CONCEPT 4 동명사의 관용 표현

go+-ing	~하러 가다
be busy+-ing	~하느라 바쁘다
feel like+-ing	~하고 싶다
How[What] about+-ing ~?	~하는 게 어때?
spend+시간/돈+-ing	~하느라 시간/돈을 쓰다
look forward to+-ing	~하기를 고대하다

Let's go hiking this weekend.

She was busy calling her friends.

I feel like going back home.

How about riding a motorcycle?

He spent a lot of money playing online games.

I'm looking forward to hearing from you.

go+-ing의 예
• go camping: 캠핑하러 가다
• go swimming: 수영하러 가다
• go fishing: 낚시하러 가다

VOCA collect 모으다 | rock 돌 | accessory 장신구 | idiot 바보 | reply 응답

Let's Check It Out

>>> 정답 16쪽

A 괄호 안의 단어를 빈칸에 알맞은 형태로 쓰시오. 각 1점

1 _____ is good for your health. (jog)

2 We enjoyed _____ in the lake. (swim)

3 My hobby is _____ cartoons. (draw)

4 I like _____ in the singing room. (sing)

5 My grandmother is good at _____. (run)

B 밑줄 친 부분을 바르게 고치시오. 각 1점

1 I enjoy <u>studing</u> at school. → _____

2 He's interested in <u>draw</u> puppies. → _____

3 The couple enjoys <u>to travel</u>. → _____

4 I finished <u>to change</u> your tires. → _____

5 <u>Skate</u> is my favorite sport. → _____

C 밑줄 친 부분의 쓰임이 [보기]와 같으면 =로, 아니면 ≠로 표시하시오. 각 1점

> 보기 The kids liked <u>baking</u> cookies.

1 My dog's favorite activity is <u>sleeping</u>. → _____

2 Surprisingly, my brother is <u>reading</u> a book. → _____

3 <u>Being</u> kind to others is great. → _____

4 She was <u>watching</u> a movie at that time. → _____

5 She is proud of <u>winning</u> the championship. → _____

D 괄호 안에 주어진 단어를 빈칸에 바르게 배열하시오. 각 1점

1 She and I _____ together. (swimming, go)

2 We _____ some rest now. (getting, like, feel)

3 She _____ her friend. (busy, was, texting)

4 I _____ business with you. (doing, to, forward, look)

5 My sister _____ her meals. (finishing, an hour, spends)

VOCA skate 스케이트 타다 | bake 굽다 | surprisingly 놀랍게도 | proud of ~을 자랑스러워하는 | win 우승하다, 이기다 | championship 대회 | get some rest 휴식하다 | business 사업 | meal 식사

★ **Ready for Exams**

>>> 정답 17쪽

My score is

Let's Check It Out _____ / 20점   0~24점 → Level 1 Test
Ready for Exams _____ / 15점 ➡ 25~29점 → Level 2 Test
Total _____ / 35점   30~35점 → Level 3 Test

1   Which is the common word for the blanks? 2점

> • Do you like _____ volleyball?
> • How about _____ soccer after school?

① play   ② to play   ③ to playing
④ playing   ⑤ plays

2   다음 중 밑줄 친 부분의 쓰임이 나머지와 다른 것은? 2점

① <u>Riding</u> on a boat is easy for me.
② She was <u>dancing</u> on the stage.
③ Dan liked <u>talking</u> about his life.
④ His hobby is <u>making</u> model airplanes.
⑤ He didn't finish <u>reading</u> the comic book.

3   어법상 어색한 것을 모두 고르시오. 2점

① I hate going shopping alone.
② He stopped rolling the paper bag.
③ Tell lies doesn't help you at all.
④ He is busy to type his report.
⑤ Her plan is go to Havana next year.

4   Find the error and correct it. 4점

> They were busy to prepare for their wedding.

_____ ➡ _____

5   그림을 보고 조건에 맞도록 빈칸을 채우시오. 5점

> • 조건 1   (A)와 (B) 둘 다 같은 형태로 쓸 것
> • 조건 2   어휘 – enjoy, sing, like, dance
> • 조건 3   주어진 어휘를 순서대로 쓰되 필요하면 어형 변화할 것

➡ The cat (A) _____ _____, and the lions

(B) _____ _____.

VOCA   model airplane 모형 비행기 | roll 말다 | type 타이핑하다 | report 보고서 | Havana 아바나(쿠바의 수도) | prepare 준비하다 | wedding 결혼(식)

UNIT 26 동명사와 to부정사

CONCEPT 1 동명사만 목적어로 취하는 동사

enjoy, mind, give up, finish, practice, stop, keep, quit, dislike

We will keep shouting.

She finished making a paper doll.

GRAMMAR POINT

like와 dislike

• like는 동명사와 to부정사 모두 목적어로 취하지만 dislike는 동명사만 목적어로 취한다.

CONCEPT 2 to부정사만 목적어로 취하는 동사

want, wish, hope, expect, plan, promise, decide, would like, learn

She hopes to go to Alaska.

I want to subscribe to this channel.

CONCEPT 3 둘 다 목적어로 취하는 동사

A 의미 차이가 거의 없는 경우

start, begin, like, love, continue, hate

Suddenly, she began crying (= to cry).

Hayashi loves singing (= to sing) K-pop.

B 의미 차이가 있는 경우

stop + to부정사

• 참고로, 'stop+to부정사'에서 to부정사는 목적어 역할을 하는 명사적 용법이 아니라 부사적 용법(목적)으로 사용된 것이다.

	+동명사	+to부정사
remember	~했던 것을 기억하다	~할 것을 기억하다
forget	~했던 것을 잊다	~할 것을 잊다
try	한번 ~해보다	~하기 위해 애쓰다
stop	~하는 것을 멈추다	~하기 위해 (하던 일을) 멈추다

I can't forget meeting you at the beach.

Mr. Ryu, don't forget to meet Mr. Lim.

Mom remembered buying our first house.

Remember to buy the blue sneakers for me.

Why don't you just try talking to her?

I tried to move the heavy box.

They stopped watching the movie on Netflix.

The old man stopped to look at the ad.

VOCA shout 소리 지르다 | paper doll 종이 인형 | subscribe to ~을 구독하다 | suddenly 갑자기 | sneakers 운동화 | ad (= advertisement) 광고

Let's Check It Out

>>> 정답 17쪽

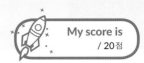

A [ ]에서 알맞은 것을 고르시오. 각 1점

1 Do you mind [to hold / holding] the door?
2 Where do you plan [to go / going]?
3 She finished [to take / taking] pictures.
4 Don't give up [to sell / selling] the car.
5 He kept [to move / moving] slowly.

B 괄호 안에 주어진 단어를 빈칸에 알맞은 형태로 쓰시오. 각 1점

1 They practiced _____ the drum. (play)
2 I hate _____ to the dentist. (go)
3 Do you want _____ for a ride? (go)
4 My grandmother quit _____. (drive)
5 We decided _____ to another city. (move)

C 밑줄 친 부분이 어색하면 바르게 고치시오. 각 1점

1 He promised to buy flowers every month.   → _____
2 The children loved take care of the cat.   → _____
3 He enjoys to listen to classical music.   → _____
4 They planned traveling across America.   → _____
5 The dog dislikes to be inside an elevator.   → _____

D 우리말과 일치하도록 빈칸을 채우시오. 각 1점

1 저 가르쳤던 거 기억나세요?
   → Do you remember _____ me?

2 그는 길을 묻기 위해 멈춰 섰다.
   → He stopped _____ for directions.

3 나는 어젯밤에 문 잠그는 것을 잊었다.
   → I forgot _____ the door last night.

4 도서관에서는 잡담을 멈춰 주세요. (chat)
   → Please stop _____ in the library.

5 Sullivan은 우선 Helen을 가르치려고 노력했다.
   → Sullivan first tried _____ Helen.

VOCA dentist 치과 의사 | go for a ride 드라이브하다 | take care of ~을 돌보다 | direction 방향 | chat 잡담하다

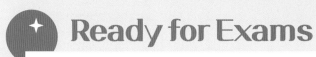

Ready for Exams

>>> 정답 17쪽

My score is

Let's Check It Out _____ / 20점   0~24점 → Level 1 Test
Ready for Exams _____ / 15점   25~29점 → Level 2 Test
Total _____ / 35점   30~35점 → Level 3 Test

1 다음 빈칸에 적절하지 <u>않은</u> 것은? 2점

> Do you _____ walking on the beach?

① love   ② mind   ③ enjoy
④ remember   ⑤ want

2 다음 중 어법상 <u>어색한</u> 문장은? 2점

① He likes driving in the countryside.
② I would like to change the plan.
③ The boy didn't give up riding his bike.
④ They finished to pack at 12:15.
⑤ He didn't stop running until midnight.

3 Which word is NOT necessary when translating the sentence? 4점

> 나는 Kane을 초대하고 싶었지만, 그에게 전화하는 것을 잊어버렸다.

① wanted   ② to invite   ③ forgot
④ calling   ⑤ him

4 그림을 보고 우리말을 영작하시오. 4점

> 나의 언니는 암벽 등반하러 가는 것을 즐겨.
> enjoy, go rock-climbing

→ _____

5 Fill in the blanks to complete the translation. 3점

> 나는 시험 때문에 게임 하는 것을 그만두었다.

→ I _____ _____ games because of the test.

VOCA   countryside 시골 | pack 짐을 싸다 | until ~까지 | midnight 자정 | rock-climbing 암벽 등반

Review Test

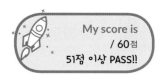

My score is
/ 60점
51점 이상 PASS!!

>>> 정답 17쪽

U25_2
01 다음 빈칸에 가장 적절한 것은? 2점

> What is your reason for _____ late today?

① be
② is
③ to being
④ are
⑤ being

U26_3A
02 Which is proper for the blank? (2 answers) 2점

> She hated _____ for a long time.

① shop
② shopping
③ shopped
④ shops
⑤ to shop

U26_1+2
03 각 빈칸에 들어갈 말이 바르게 짝지어진 것은? 2점

 한눈에 쏙

> • Do you mind _____ the window?
> • She hopes _____ her house.

① closing – selling
② to close – selling
③ closing – to sell
④ to close – to sell
⑤ close – sell

U26_3B
04 다음 중 짝지어진 두 문장의 의미가 <u>다른</u> 것은? 2점

 한눈에 쏙

① He is good at speaking Spanish.
= He speaks Spanish well.
② How about trying Vietnamese food?
= Why don't we try Vietnamese food?
③ She went to the lake to fish.
= She went fishing at the lake.
④ I stopped to talk to a police officer.
= I stopped talking to a police officer.
⑤ We love going camping on weekends.
= We love to go camping on weekends.

U25_2+GP+U26_2
05 Whose translation is correct? 2점

> 수영을 배우는 것은 어렵니?

① 재훈: Is to swim learning hard?
② 유리: Is swimming learn hard?
③ 준서: Is to learn swimming hard?
④ 상민: Is learning swim hard?
⑤ 민아: Is learning to swim hard?

U25_3
06 밑줄 친 부분의 쓰임이 나머지와 <u>다른</u> 하나는? 2점

① She is interested in <u>growing</u> plants.
② He began <u>studying</u> science harder.
③ Her hobby is <u>cooking</u> Thai food.
④ <u>Traveling</u> by airplane is fun.
⑤ Her brother was <u>sleeping</u> on the sofa.

U25_2+4+GP
07 다음 중 어법상 <u>어색한</u> 것은? 2점

함정

① Hyemi finished writing her report.
② I'm looking forward to hear from you.
③ We went swimming every Sunday.
④ I really enjoy driving in the rain.
⑤ Eating too much sugar is bad for your health.

U25_4
08 다음 중 어법상 옳은 문장으로 묶인 것은? 3점

★ 고난도

> ⓐ He was so busy at meeting new people.
> ⓑ Driving to Gwangju took 8 hours.
> ⓒ We always enjoy going to the movies.
> ⓓ She felt like to have cool *naengmyeon*.
> ⓔ Why don't we go shopping together?

① ⓐ, ⓒ
② ⓐ, ⓒ, ⓔ
③ ⓑ, ⓒ
④ ⓑ, ⓒ, ⓔ
⑤ ⓒ, ⓓ, ⓔ

U25_1+2

09 밑줄 친 동명사의 쓰임을 고르고, 문장을 해석하시오.
각 2점

> Did you finish underlined{painting} the roof?

(1) 쓰임 ➡ (주어 / 목적어 / 보어)

(2) 해석 ➡ _____

U25_2

10 Fill in the blank to make the two sentences have the same meaning. 4점

> Jade speaks Russian very well.

➡ Jade is very good at _____ Russian.

U25_4

11 우리말과 일치하도록 주어진 단어를 활용하여 문장을 완성하시오. 4점

> 아빠는 부엌에서 아침 식사를 준비하시느라 바쁘시다.

➡ My dad _____ _____
_____ breakfast in the kitchen.
(busy, prepare)

U25_2

12 다음은 남성용 마스크팩의 광고 문구이다. 어법상 어색한 부분을 찾아서 바르게 고치시오. 4점

Have healthy skin is not just for women.

_____ ➡ _____

U26_2+3A

13 다음 두 문장 중 어색한 것을 찾아 바르게 고치시오. 4점

> ⓐ What would you like having, ma'am?
> ⓑ Daniel loves having Peking duck.

( ) _____ ➡ _____

U18_2+U19_1D+U25_1

14 ★고난도 다음 문장에서 어법상 어색한 부분을 모두 찾아 바르게 고치시오. (정답 최대 3개) 7점

> Much people think they know their friends good, so they stop to try to maintain their friendship.

➡ _____
_____

U25_2

15 어휘와 힌트를 이용하여 우리말을 영작하시오. 6점

> 모두가 그녀의 불평을 듣는 데 질렸다.
> ·어휘 hear, complaints, everybody
> ·힌트 be tired of: ~에 질리다

➡ _____

U25_4

16 다음 문장에서 어법상 어색한 곳을 찾아 바르게 고치시오. 4점

> The government is going to spend $1,000,000 to build the bridge over the sea.

_____ ➡ _____

U04_2+U26_3B

17 👁한눈에쏙 Look at the picture and complete the dialog by using the verb "lock." 각 3점

 Oh, my. Did you (A) _____ the door in the morning?

 Of course. I clearly remember (B) _____ the door!

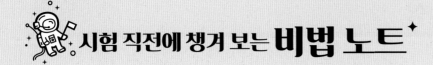

시험 직전에 챙겨 보는 **비법 노트**

>>> 정답 17쪽

한눈에 쏙! 아래 노트를 보면서 빈칸을 채워 보세요.

1 동명사 vs. 현재분사

	형태	역할
동명사	-ing	주어, 1)_____, 2)_____
현재분사	3)_____	진행형

2 동명사 vs. to부정사

① 동명사만 목적어로 취하는 동사	1)e_____, 2)m____, 3)g____u__, 4)f_____, 5)p_____ 등
② to부정사만 목적어로 취하는 동사	6)wə___, 7)wi___, 8)h____, 9)e_____, 10)p____, 11)p_____ 등
③ 둘 다 목적어로 취하는 동사	12)s_____, 13)b_____, 14)li___, 15)lo___, 16)c_____, 17)h____ 등

3 ★ 뒤에 오는 말에 따라 의미가 달라지는 동사

동사	+to부정사	+-ing
1)_____/2)_____	~할 것을 잊다/기억하다	~했던 것을 잊다/기억하다
3)_____	~하기 위해 애쓰다	한번 ~해보다
4)_____	~하기 위해 멈추다	~하는 것을 멈추다

헷갈리지 말자! 초록색으로 표시된 부분을 바르게 고쳐 쓰세요.

1 We are looking forward to <u>meet</u> you soon.

2 The girl finished <u>to make</u> a paper rose.

3 The bus stopped <u>picking</u> up the students.

CHAPTER 10
문장의 형식

UNIT 27 There is 구문, 2형식(감각동사)

1 There is/are 구문

「There is/are+주어 ~」는 '~(들)이 있다'라는 뜻으로 be동사 다음에 오는 명사가 주어이며, 주어의 수에 따라 be동사의 형태가 결정된다.

긍정문	There is+단수 주어 ~. There are+복수 주어 ~.	There is a moon in the sky. There are a lot of people on the street.
부정문	There is/are not ~.	There is not[isn't] a moon in the sky. There are not[aren't] many people on the street.
의문문	Is/Are there ~? – Yes, there is/are. – No, there isn't/aren't.	Is there a moon in the sky? – Yes, there is. / No, there isn't. Are there a lot of people on the street? – Yes, there are. / No, there aren't.
과거형	There was+단수 주어 ~. There were+복수 주어 ~.	There was a princess long ago. There were seven dwarfs.

2 2형식: 감각동사 + 형용사(주격 보어)

감각동사 look, feel, sound, smell, taste 뒤에 주격 보어로 형용사가 쓰인 2형식 문장으로, '~하게 …하다'라고 해석한다.

look	~하게 보이다		You look tall.
feel	~하게 느끼다		I feel sad.
sound	~하게 들리다	+ 형용사	That sounds good.
smell	~한 냄새가 나다		This jam smells delicious.
taste	~한 맛이 나다		The snack tastes salty.

GRAMMAR POINT

There is/are 구문의 주어

- much, many, a lot of, (a) little, (a) few, some 등 주어에 수량을 나타내는 말이 있을 때는 이어지는 명사가 단수인지 복수인지를 살펴본다.

  There is a lot of water in my glass.

  There are few students in the classroom.

  Was there any surprising news?

부사 there

- there는 '거기에, 거기로'라는 뜻의 부사로도 쓰인다.

  See you there.

  (거기서 보자.)

  They went there again.

  (그들은 거기로 다시 갔다.)

감각동사의 보어

- 감각동사의 보어로 부사를 사용하지 않는다.

  The bridge looks safely. (×)
  → The bridge looks safe. (○)

  The coffee smells well. (×)
  → The coffee smells good. (○)

감각동사 + like + 명사

- 감각동사 뒤에 명사를 사용하려면 「감각동사+like+명사」로 나타낸다.

  The baby tiger looks like a cat.

  (아기 호랑이가 고양이처럼 보인다.)

  His lie sounds like the truth.

  (그의 거짓말은 사실처럼 들린다.)

  The tofu tastes like real beef.

  (그 두부는 진짜 쇠고기 맛이 난다.)

VOCA   moon 달 | princess 공주 | dwarf 난쟁이 | glass 유리잔 | surprising 놀라운 | bridge 다리 | safe 안전한 | lie 거짓말 | truth 사실 | tofu 두부 | beef 쇠고기

A [ ]에서 알맞은 것을 고르시오. 각 1점

1 There [is / are] a tiger behind you.

2 [Is / Are] there many sheep in the field?

3 There [is / are] no sun in the sky today.

4 There [is / are] many differences between us.

5 There [is / are] lots of snow outside.

6 There [was / were] several fish in his bucket.

B 문장을 괄호 안의 지시대로 바꾸어 쓸 때 빈칸에 알맞은 말을 쓰시오. 각 1점

1 There is a bird in the cage. (부정문)

→ _____ _____ a bird in the cage.

2 There are lots of fish in the fish tank. (의문문)

→ _____ _____ lots of fish in the fish tank?

3 There is a bad queen. (과거형)

→ _____ _____ a bad queen.

C [ ]에서 알맞은 것을 고르시오. 각 1점

1 She looked [sad / sadly].

2 That sounds [good / well].

3 It [smells / smells like] a cookie.

4 This [tastes / tastes like] a melon.

5 Did he feel [happy / happily]?

D 우리말과 같은 뜻이 되도록 빈칸에 알맞은 말을 쓰시오. 각 1점

1 레몬은 신맛이 난다.

→ The lemon _____ sour.

2 그 소년은 영화배우처럼 생겼다.

→ The boy looks _____ a movie star.

3 그의 목소리는 부드럽게 들린다.

→ His voice sounds _____.

4 나는 바보 같은 느낌이 든다.

→ I _____ _____ a fool.

VOCA behind ~ 뒤에 | difference 차이 | bucket 양동이 | cage 우리 | fish tank 어항 | sour 신

🚀 **My score is**

Let's Check It Out _____ / 18점   0~21점 → Level 1 Test
Ready for Exams _____ / 12점 ➡ 22~25점 → Level 2 Test
Total _____ / 30점   26~30점 → Level 3 Test

1 Which sentences are grammatically <u>wrong</u>? (Find ALL.) 3점

  ① There is hot springs in New Zealand.

  ② There was a wide river around here.

  ③ Are there no questions about it?

  ④ There weren't any hope.

  ⑤ Were there many peaches on the tree?

2 다음 그림에 대한 설명이 <u>잘못된</u> 것은? 3점

  ① There is a princess.

  ② There are seven dwarfs.

  ③ There are two deer beside the princess.

  ④ There are rabbits in front of the dwarfs.

  ⑤ There is a blue bird.

3 빈칸에 들어갈 말로 알맞지 <u>않은</u> 것을 고르시오. 2점

> This speaker sounds _____.

  ① good   ② great   ③ noisy

  ④ better   ⑤ loudly

4 다음 중 어법상 옳은 문장을 만들 수 <u>없는</u> 것은? 4점

  ① smell / bad / Does / it / ?

  ② looks / . / really / tired / He

  ③ plan / a / . / It / sounds / perfect

  ④ feels / good / . / The / blanket / so

  ⑤ sweet / didn't / taste / The / . / grape

VOCA hot spring 온천 | peach 복숭아 | deer 사슴 | blanket 담요

UNIT 28 4형식(수여동사), 5형식

 4형식(수여동사)

수여동사란 목적어를 두 개 가지는 동사를 말하며 'A(간접 목적어)에게 B(직접 목적어)를 ~해주다'라는 뜻으로 해석한다.

주어	수여동사	간접 목적어	직접 목적어
I	showed	him	a picture.
Dad	makes	me	spaghetti.
Ms. Kim	asked	us	hard questions.

 수여동사의 문장 변환

「수여동사＋직접 목적어＋전치사(to, for, of)＋간접 목적어」로 바꿔 쓸 수 있다.

> 4형식: 수여동사＋간접 목적어(~에게) ＋직접 목적어(…을)
> → 3형식: 수여동사＋직접 목적어(…을)＋전치사(to, for, of)＋간접 목적어(~에게)

4형식에서 3형식으로 바꿀 때 동사에 따라 전치사를 달리 쓴다.

to를 사용하는 동사	give, bring, lend, send, sell, show, teach, write, hand
for를 사용하는 동사	make, buy, cook, get, find
of를 사용하는 동사	ask

He gave me flowers. → He gave flowers to me.

Will you buy me a new phone? → Will you buy a new phone for me?

Can I ask you a question? → Can I ask a question of you?

 5형식

「주어＋동사＋목적어＋목적격 보어」로 쓰이고 목적격 보어로는 형용사, 명사 또는 to부정사가 올 수 있다.

주어	동사	목적어	목적격 보어
Everybody	called	him	Mr. Grumpy. (명사)
The song	made	us	happy. (형용사)
He	told	me	to wait outside. (to부정사)

GRAMMAR POINT

간접 목적어와 직접 목적어

- 「간접 목적어(사람)＋직접 목적어(사물)」와 「직접 목적어(사물)＋전치사＋간접 목적어(사람)」의 위치를 잘 파악한다.

  My brother taught math me. (×)

  My brother taught me math. (○)

- 4형식의 경우 직접 목적어 자리에 대명사를 쓸 수 없다.

  Show me it. (×)

  → Show it to me. (○)

  → Show me the ticket. (○)

명사를 목적격 보어로 취하는 동사

- call, name, make, elect, consider 등

형용사를 목적격 보어로 취하는 동사

- make, keep(유지하다), find(여기다), consider(여기다) 등

- 목적격 보어에 부사를 쓰지 않음에 유의한다.

  He made us sadly. (×)

to부정사를 목적격 보어로 취하는 동사

- want, ask, tell, teach, expect, would like, advise, allow, order 등

VOCA show 보여주다 | bring 가져다주다 | lend 빌려주다 | sell 팔다 | hand 건네주다 | get 가져다주다 | find 찾아주다 | outside 밖에서

Let's Check It Out

>>> 정답 18쪽

A [ ]에서 알맞은 것을 고르시오. 각 1점

1 I showed [him / to him] the answer.

2 Josh gave [a letter Jane / Jane a letter].

3 Did she send [him it / it to him]?

4 Ice cream makes us [happily / happy].

5 She asked him [speak / to speak] more clearly.

B 다음 문장을 바꿔 쓸 때 [ ]에서 알맞은 것을 고르시오. 각 1점

1 Hand me the gun.

　→ Hand the gun [for / to / by] me.

2 She brought him a glass of water.

　→ She brought a glass of water [to / by / of] him.

3 Will you find me a coin?

　→ Will you find a coin [to / for / of] me?

4 You can ask me any questions.

　→ You can ask any questions [to / for / of] me.

C 빈칸에 알맞은 전치사를 [보기]에서 골라 쓰시오. 각 1점

보기	to	for	of

1 I can lend some money _____ you.

2 Brian bought a cake _____ his kid.

3 I sold my car _____ James.

4 Did you cook a nice dinner _____ Mom?

5 May I ask a favor _____ you?

D 밑줄 친 부분이 어색하면 바르게 고치시오. 각 1점

1 His speech made me <u>sleepily</u>.　　　　→ _____

2 I found your story very <u>touching</u>.　　　→ _____

3 The old man told me <u>staying</u> back.　　→ _____

4 Everybody was expecting you <u>to come</u> back.　→ _____

5 I can't allow you <u>marry</u> my daughter.　　→ _____

VOCA　favor 호의, 부탁 | speech 연설 | touching 감동적인 | stay back 물러서다 | marry ~와 결혼하다

1   다음 중 어법상 어색한 것은? 2점

① We named the dog Indiana.
② This will keep you awake.
③ We had to ask him to leave.
④ Don't make me uncomfortably.
⑤ He ordered everyone to stop.

2   다음 빈칸에 들어갈 말로 적절한 것은? (답 2개) 2점

I don't _____ myself successful.

① find   ② name   ③ allow
④ advise   ⑤ consider

3   Which is NOT correct for at least one of the blanks? 3점

ⓐ She will _____ a package to me.
ⓑ Did you _____ yesterday's homework to me?
ⓒ David didn't _____ his test paper to the teacher.

① give   ② show   ③ send
④ get   ⑤ hand

4   Rearrange the words correctly according to the picture. 4점

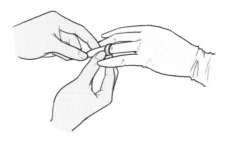

the groom, the bride, gives, a ring

→ _____

VOCA   awake 깨어 있는 | uncomfortably 불편하게 | successful 성공한 | package 소포, 택배 | test paper 시험지 | groom 신랑 | bride 신부

>>> 정답 18쪽

U27_1

01 Which is the correct phrase for the blank? 2점

> A: How many boats are there on the sea?
> B: _____ five boats.

① They are
② There is
③ It is
④ There are
⑤ That is

U27_1

02 다음 우리말과 같은 의미의 문장은? 2점

> 거리에 많은 차들이 있었니?

① There are many cars on the street?
② Are there many cars on the street?
③ Was there lots of cars on the street?
④ Were there lots of cars on the street?
⑤ There were lots of cars on the street?

U27_2+GP

03 다음 빈칸에 알맞지 않은 것은? 2점

> The fusion food tasted _____.

① good
② deliciously
③ terrible
④ spicy
⑤ sour

U27_2+GP

04 다음 중 어법상 옳은 문장을 2개 고르시오. 3점

 고난도
① A fox fur coat feels smoothly.
② Your English sounds like a native's.
③ The potato chip tastes salty.
④ Did the party look greatly?
⑤ The room doesn't smell well.

U28_3+GP

05 다음 중 어법상 어색한 것을 바르게 고친 것은? (정답 최대 3개) 2점

> I would like you doing big something for our country.

① would → must
② like → liking
③ you → your
④ doing → to do
⑤ big something → something big

U28_3+GP

06 Which is proper for the blank? (Find ALL.) 2점

> I _____ him to carry the box.

① want
② asked
③ will tell
④ named
⑤ didn't expect

U28_1+2

07 다음 중 어법상 어색한 문장은? 2점

 함정
① The girl lent him a USB memory stick.
② She bought a CD for her son.
③ Can I ask a favor of you?
④ Mom gave some advice for me.
⑤ They showed the house to me.

U28_2

08 Which describes the picture correctly? (2 answers) 2점

① They are giving some food the poor.
② Some food is giving to the poor.
③ They are giving some food to the poor.
④ They are giving the poor some food.
⑤ They are giving some food for the poor.

U27_1

09 Translate the Korean into English according to the conditions. 5점

> 신문에 무슨 재미있는 기사라도 있어요?
>
> ·Condition 1   어휘 – interesting, newspaper, there, news, any
> ·Condition 2   8단어로 쓸 것

➜ _____

U27_2+GP

10 다음 두 문장이 같도록 빈칸에 알맞은 말을 쓰시오. 4점

> Duncan looks gentle.

➜ Duncan looks _____ a gentleman.

U27_2

11 다음 그림을 설명할 수 있는 문장을 완성하시오. 4점

> ·어휘   sleep, look
> ·조건   필요하면 어휘를 변형할 것

➜ The kid _____ .

U28_2

12 다음 두 문장의 의미가 같도록 빈칸을 채우시오. 4점

> My niece made me a necklace.

➜ My niece made _____ .

U28_2

13 다음 단어들을 배열하여 문장을 만드시오. 4점

> I'd, like, you, cook, to, *kimbap*, for

➜ _____

U27_2+GP

14 Rewrite the sentence correctly. 4점

> *Songpyeon* looks a half moon.

➜ _____

U28_3+GP

15 다음 조건에 맞게 우리말을 영작하시오. 6점

고난도

> 누가 너에게 읽고 쓰는 것을 가르쳤느냐?
>
> ·어휘   teach
> ·조건 1   필요 시 어형 변화할 것
> ·조건 2   7단어로 쓸 것

➜ _____

U28_2

16 주어진 단어들을 이용하여 우리말을 영작하시오. 4점

> 할아버지가 나에게 시계를 사주셨다.
> my grandfather, a watch, buy

➜ _____

U28_2

17 빈칸에 공통으로 들어갈 말을 쓰시오. 4점

> • My brothers sometimes _____ a kite for me.
> • He will _____ a great archer.

➜ _____

U28_3+GP

18 어법상 어색한 부분을 찾아 바르게 고치시오. 4점

> You can't expect them be perfect. Nobody is perfect.

_____ ➜ _____

한눈에 쏙! 아래 노트를 보면서 빈칸을 채워 보세요.

1 2형식 : 감각동사+형용사

(look, sound, smell, taste) + (1) _____ *)

*부사는 안 됨

2 4형식(수여동사)

(S) + (V) + (IO (간·목)) + (DO (직·목))

(S) + (V) + (DO) + (전치사) + (IO)

→ 대부분 → to
buy, make, get → 1) _____
ask → 2) _____

3 5형식

(S) + (V) + (O (목적어)) + (OC (목적격 보어))

→ 1) _____ , 명사, to부정사

헷갈리지 말자! 초록색으로 표시된 부분을 바르게 고쳐 쓰세요.

1 I feel sadly.

2 Will you buy a new phone to me?

3 Don't expect me be your friend.

CHAPTER 11

전치사와 접속사

시간 전치사, 장소 전치사

1 시간 전치사

at(~에)	시각, 정오, 일출, 일몰과 같은 때의 한 시점	Do you usually have lunch at noon?
on(~에)	날짜, 요일, 특정한 날	We eat rice cake soup on New Year's Day.
in(~에)	월, 연도, 계절, 오전, 오후	He was born in 2010.
until(~까지)	동작, 상태의 계속 (= till)	He will wait until 10 o'clock.
by(~까지)	동작의 완료	You should finish the work by tomorrow.
for(~ 동안)	구체적인 지속 기간	They will stay here for seven days.
during (~ 중에, 동안)	사건, 특정한 기간	What is your plan during summer vacation?

2 장소 전치사

at(~에)	비교적 좁은 장소	He is waiting for you at the bus stop.
in(~에)	넓은 지역, ~ 안에	There are many festivals in Europe.
on(~ 위에)	접촉되어	Mom put the dish on the table.
by(~ 옆에)	(= next to = beside)	Marie sits by[next to, beside] me.
over(~ 위에)	수직으로 바로 위	Look at the bridge over the river.
under(~ 밑에)	수직으로 바로 밑	I found the toy under the bed.
behind(~ 뒤에)	(↔ in front of)	The sun disappeared behind the clouds.

3 기타 전치사

교통수단	by(~을 타고)	We go to school by subway.
방향	into(~ 안으로) out of(~ 밖으로) along(~을 따라서) across from(~의 맞은편에) through(~을 통과하여)	Throw the ball into the box. Take the book out of your bag. She walked along the road. There is a bank across from the library. We took a walk through the park.

VOCA noon 정오 | rice cake soup 떡국 | New Year's Day 설날 | be born 태어나다 | plan 계획 | dish 접시 | disappear 사라지다 | cloud 구름

Let's Check It Out

>>> 정답 19쪽

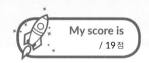

A [ ]에서 알맞은 것을 고르시오. 각 1점

1 There is lots of frozen food [at / in] the refrigerator.

2 You must stay here [by / until] tomorrow.

3 You can see the stars [in / at] night.

4 He works from 8 a.m. [to / by] 5 p.m.

5 I will visit Singapore [for / during] my vacation.

6 I was in the hospital [for / during] three days.

7 We went to New York [on / in] 2008.

8 What does he usually do [on / in] the evening?

B 빈칸에 알맞은 전치사를 [보기]에서 골라 쓰시오. 각 1점

보기	in	at	on

1 He lived _____ Sanbon.

2 My grandma gets up _____ 6 o'clock.

3 It snows _____ winter.

4 Let's meet _____ the front door.

5 I always drink milk _____ the morning.

6 Put the books _____ the shelf.

C 우리말에 맞게 빈칸에 알맞은 말을 쓰시오. 각 1점

1 우리는 자전거를 타고 일하러 간다
   → We go to work _____ bike.

2 그의 꿈은 실크로드를 따라 여행하는 것이다.
   → His dream is to travel _____ the Silk Road.

3 그녀의 집 뒤에는 높은 울타리가 있었다.
   → There was a high fence _____ her house.

4 그녀는 나무 아래 서 있었다.
   → She was standing _____ the tree.

5 헨젤과 그레텔은 숲을 통과하여 걸어갔다.
   → Hansel and Gretel walked _____ the forest.

VOCA frozen 냉동된 | refrigerator 냉장고 | Singapore 싱가포르 | front door 정문 | shelf 선반 | Silk Road 실크로드(고대 동서양의 무역로) | fence 울타리, 담장

UNIT 29   141

1 다음 빈칸에 공통으로 들어갈 전치사는? 2점

> • I don't drink coffee _____ night.
> • The library closes _____ 9:30.
> • Let's eat _____ a fast-food restaurant.

① in   ② on   ③ by
④ at   ⑤ after

2 다음 중 빈칸에 'on'을 쓸 수 <u>없는</u> 것은? 2점

① I was sleeping _____ midnight.
② Field Day is _____ May 3.
③ We go to church _____ Sundays.
④ Hang the picture _____ the wall.
⑤ Girls give boys chocolate _____ Valentine's Day.

3 Which sentence or sentences are <u>incorrect</u>? 2점

> ⓐ Let's have lunch in noon.
> ⓑ She studied for the test until midnight.
> ⓒ I lived in Tokyo for two years.
> ⓓ The reporter met Willy on the airport.

4 다음 그림에 맞게 영어로 문장을 완성하시오. 3점

> 그 산 위에 무지개가 있다. (rainbow)

➡ There is _____ .

5 Fill in the blank with <u>1 word</u> so that the two sentences have the same meaning. 2점

> The bank is next to the stationery store.

➡ The bank is _____ the stationery store.

VOCA   close 닫다 | midnight 자정, 한밤중 | reporter 기자 | stationery store 문방구

142

등위 접속사, 종속 접속사

1 등위 접속사

등위 접속사는 단어, 구 또는 절을 대등한 관계로 연결한다.

and(~와, 그리고)	단어와 단어	I want a banana and a strawberry.
	구와 구	My hobbies are gardening and singing songs.
	절과 절	I am in the room, and she is in the kitchen.
or(또는, 혹은)	단어와 단어	You or your friend must go there.
	구와 구	He went there by bus or on foot.
	절과 절	Let's play games, or let's go shopping.
but(그러나)	단어와 단어	He is poor but happy.
	절과 절	It was not my fault, but it was God's will.
so(그래서)	절과 절	He got up late, so he was late for school.

2 종속 접속사

종속 접속사는 주절과 종속절을 이어준다.

that(~라는 것, ~라고)	문장 안에서 주어, 보어, 목적어 역할을 하는 명사절을 이끈다.	
	주어	That Bora likes Seho is true.
	보어	My hope is that Bin likes me.
	목적어	I don't believe (that) he is a millionaire.
when(~할 때)	부사절(종속절), 주절 = 주절+종속절	
	When I was young, I lived in the country. = I lived in the country when I was young.	
because(~하기 때문에)	Because it was raining, we didn't go out. = We didn't go out because it was raining.	
if(~한다면)	If the weather is fine, I will go on a picnic. = I will go on a picnic if the weather is fine.	

VOCA strawberry 딸기 | garden 정원을 가꾸다 | fault 잘못 | God 신 | will 의지, 뜻 | millionaire 백만장자 | pass 통과하다, 합격하다 | monster 괴물

A 빈칸에 알맞은 접속사를 [보기]에서 골라 쓰시오. 각 1점

> 보기   and   but   or

1 Harry _____ I are classmates.

2 I didn't have breakfast, _____ I'm not hungry.

3 Sit down _____ tell me about your trip.

4 Grapes are usually green _____ red.

5 He is old _____ fast.

B 빈칸에 알맞은 접속사를 [보기]에서 골라 쓰시오. 각 1점

> 보기   because   if   so

1 He was in pain, _____ he went to see a doctor.

2 He is very popular _____ he is a movie star.

3 _____ you are free, come to the party.

4 I borrowed some money from my friend, _____ I bought some milk.

5 I'll call you _____ you give me your phone number.

C 빈칸에 'that' 또는 'when' 중에서 알맞은 것을 쓰시오. 각 1점

1 She knows _____ he won't come.

2 _____ I came back, no one was home.

3 I thought _____ the stars were talking to me.

4 Don't drive _____ you are sleepy.

5 _____ she went to Harvard is true.

6 _____ your father was little, he was so cute.

D 빈칸에 알맞은 말을 [보기]에서 고르시오. 각 1점

> 보기   ⓐ so I like it   ⓑ but it is hard to climb   ⓒ if you're busy now

1 We can meet later _____.

2 English is interesting, _____.

3 That mountain is not high, _____.

VOCA classmate 같은 반 친구 | trip 여행 | in pain 고통스러워하는 | borrow 빌리다 | Harvard 하버드 대학교

My score is

Let's Check It Out _____ / 19점   0~24점 → Level 1 Test
Ready for Exams _____ / 16점   ➡ 25~29점 → Level 2 Test
Total _____ / 35점   30~35점 → Level 3 Test

Ready for Exams

>>> 정답 20쪽

---

1 다음 빈칸에 알맞은 것은? 2점

> _____ the weather is nice on Sunday, I will do the laundry.

① If   ② And   ③ How
④ So   ⑤ Or

---

2 다음 빈칸에 공통으로 알맞은 것은? 2점

> • Hurry up, _____ you will miss the bus.
> • Is he Japanese _____ Chinese?

① and   ② but   ③ or
④ so   ⑤ that

---

3 How many sentences are natural? 3점

> ⓐ The four seasons are spring, summer, fall, or winter.
> ⓑ Sam and I are good listeners.
> ⓒ David lives in Rome, but he works there.
> ⓓ I was tired because I got some rest.

① none   ② one   ③ two
④ three   ⑤ four

---

4 Write the common word for the blanks. 4점

> • I think _____ he can solve this problem.
> • _____ Mr. Smith is a secret agent is true.

→ _____.

---

5 그림을 보고 자연스러운 의미가 되도록 다음 두 문장을 연결하시오. 5점

> He studies hard. He will take a test tomorrow.

→ _____

VOCA   do the laundry 빨래하다 | get some rest 휴식을 취하다 | secret agent 비밀 요원 | take a test 시험을 보다

Review Test

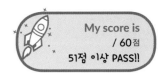

>>> 정답 20쪽

01 U29_1
다음 각 빈칸에 알맞은 말이 순서대로 나열된 것은? 2점

- I have history class _____ Tuesday.
- We will go on vacation _____ July.
- Where did you live _____ 2020?

① on – in – at
② on – in – in
③ in – on – at
④ on – in – with
⑤ in – in – with

02 U29_1+2
Which is the common word for the blanks? 2점

- I was with my children _____ that time.
- The train leaves _____ 9 o'clock.
- I met him _____ the shopping mall.

① on
② at
③ to
④ in
⑤ after

03 U29_1+2
Which sentence is incorrect? (Find ALL.) 2점

① He usually studies at night.
② Isabella sits next me.
③ What did you do in Christmas Day?
④ Is there a map on the wall?
⑤ Are there many shops in 5th Avenue?

04 U30_2+GP
다음 중 밑줄 친 'When[when]'의 뜻이 나머지와 다른 것은? 2점

① When I'm tired, I always listen to music.
② When she first met him, she didn't like him.
③ When did you start writing songs?
④ She stays at the same hotel when she goes to Busan.
⑤ When I am late, I go to school by taxi.

05 U30_1
다음 빈칸에 알맞은 것을 고르시오. 2점

Which do you like better, summer _____ winter?

① or
② and
③ but
④ so
⑤ that

06 U29_3
다음 그림을 영어로 잘 표현한 문장은? 2점

① The river runs on the city.
② The river runs through the city.
③ The city is over the river.
④ The city is under the river.
⑤ The river is across from the city.

07 U30_2
빈칸에 공통으로 들어가기에 알맞은 것은? 2점

- The fact is _____ he didn't do it.
- I think _____ she will agree with me.

① and
② to
③ that
④ after
⑤ when

08 U30_2
다음 문장의 빈칸에 알맞은 것은? 2점

Cindy studies graphic design _____ she wants to make her own homepage.

① like
② but
③ that
④ because
⑤ what

146

09 U29_1
다음 빈칸에 들어갈 말을 쓰시오. 3점

> _____ Children's Day, my parents bought a winter coat for me.

10 U29_1+GP
다음 문장에서 <u>어색한</u> 부분을 찾아 바르게 고치시오. 4점

> We played in the snow during two hours.

_____ ➝ _____

11 U29_3
다음 우리말에 맞게 빈칸에 알맞은 말을 쓰시오. 3점

> 트럭들이 고속도로를 따라 이동하고 있다.

➝ Trucks are moving _____ the highway.

12 U29_2
Translate the following Korean sentence into English. 4점
한눈에 쏙

> 나는 시드니에 있는 공항에서 그를 봤다.

➝ I saw him _____ the airport _____ Sydney.

13 U29_3
주어진 문장과 같은 의미가 되도록 빈칸에 알맞은 말을 쓰시오. 3점

> My family went to Jeju-do on an airplane.

➝ My family went to Jeju-do _____ airplane.

14 U30_1+2
Complete the sentence so that it has the same meaning as the given sentence. 4점

> I turned on the air conditioner because it was very hot.

➝ It was very hot, _____ I turned on the air conditioner.

15 U29_2
괄호 안의 단어를 이용해서 우리말을 영작하시오. 4점

> 태양이 구름 뒤에 있다. (the cloud)

➝ _____

16 U30_2+GP
빈칸에 알맞은 말을 써서 영작을 완성하시오. 5점

> 내일 비가 오면 너는 무엇을 할 거니?

➝ _____ will you do _____ it _____ tomorrow?

17 U30_1
대화가 자연스럽도록 빈칸에 알맞은 말을 쓰시오. 4점

> A: Do you live in Donghae?
> B: No, _____ I was born there.

18 U30_2
두 빈칸에 공통으로 들어갈 접속사를 쓰시오. 4점

> The neighbor said, "So you worry _____ it rains, and you worry _____ it doesn't?"

➝ _____

19 U30_1
조건에 맞게 두 문장을 한 문장으로 쓰시오. 6점
함정

> Come home early. Then, you'll be able to watch the soap opera.
> ·조건 1   조건절을 문장 앞에 쓸 것
> ·조건 2   접속사와 주어를 추가할 것

➝ _____
_____

한눈에 쏙! 아래 노트를 보면서 빈칸을 채워 보세요.

1 시간 전치사+명사

in	큰 단위	in July, in summer, in 2022
1)_____	하루를 기준으로	on Christmas Day, on Monday
at	작은 단위	at noon, at 9 p.m.

2 접속사+단어/구/문장

• that(~라는 것, ~라고): 문장을 명사로 만드는 것

① 주어	That Bora likes Seho is true.
② 보어	My guess is 1)_____ Bora likes Seho.
③ 2)_____	I don't believe that Bora likes Seho.

헷갈리지 말자! 초록색으로 표시된 부분을 바르게 고쳐 쓰세요.

1 My birthday is in June 15.

2 The shop will be closed during seven days.

3 They arrived by the taxi.

4 When he will arrive here, I will leave.

5 If the weather will be nice on Sunday, I will go on a picnic.

불규칙 동사 변화표

불규칙 동사도 외우는 방법이 있다!

1 A – A – A 형태 동일

★표시는 필수 기본 동사들

원형	뜻	과거
broadcast	방송하다	broadcast
bet	돈을 걸다	bet
burst	파열하다	burst
cast	던지다	cast
cost	비용이 들다	cost
★cut	자르다	cut
forecast	예고하다	forecast
★hit	치다	hit
hurt	아프게 하다	hurt
let	~하게 하다	let
★put	놓다	put
quit	~을 그만두다	quit
★read	읽다	read [red]
rid	~을 제거하다	rid
set	놓다	set
shed	흘리다	shed
shut	닫다	shut
spit	침을 뱉다	spit
split	쪼개다	split
spread	펴다	spread
thrust	찌르다	thrust
upset	뒤엎다	upset

2 A – A – A' 과거분사만 살짝 바뀜

원형	뜻	과거
beat	때리다, 이기다	beat

3 A – B – A 과거형에서 모음만 바뀜

원형	뜻	과거
★come	오다	came
★become	되다	became
★run	달리다	ran

4 A – B – A' 과거형은 모음 변화, 과거분사형은 원형에 –n 붙임

원형	뜻	과거
arise [əráiz]	(일이) 일어나다	arose [əróuz]
＊be (am, is, are)	~이다	was, were
blow	불다	blew [bluː]
＊do, does	하다	did
draw	당기다, 그리다	drew [druː]
＊drive	운전하다	drove [drouv]
＊eat	먹다	ate
fall	떨어지다	fell
forbid	금지하다	forbade
forgive	용서하다	forgave
forsake	그만두다, 저버리다	forsook
＊give	주다	gave [ɡeiv]
＊go	가다	went [went]
＊grow	자라다	grew [ɡruː]
＊know	알다	knew [njuː]
ride	(차, 말 등을) 타다	rode [roud]
rise	일어서다	rose [rouz]
＊see	보다	saw [sɔː]
shake	흔들다	shook [ʃuk]
show	보여주다, 보이다	showed
sow [sou]	(씨를) 뿌리다	sowed [soud]
strive	노력하다	strove [strouv]
＊take	잡다	took [tuk]
thrive	번영하다	throve [θrouv], thrived
＊throw	던지다	threw [θruː]
withdraw	물러나다	withdrew [wiðdrúː]
＊write	쓰다	wrote [rout]

5 A – B – B 원형에 –t 붙임

원형	뜻	과거
bend	구부리다	bent
＊build	세우다	built
burn	태우다	burnt, burned
deal	다루다	dealt [delt]
dwell	거주하다, 살다	dwelt, dwelled
lend	빌려주다	lent
mean	의미하다	meant [ment]
＊send	보내다	sent
smell	냄새 맡다, 냄새가 나다	smelt, smelled

spend	소비하다	spent
spoil	망쳐놓다	spoilt, spoiled

6 A – B – B 원형의 자음 + ought/aught

원형	뜻	과거
*bring	가져오다	brought [brɔːt]
*buy	사다	bought [bɔːt]
*catch	잡다	caught [kɔːt]
*fight	싸우다	fought [fɔːt]
seek	찾다	sought [sɔːt]
*teach	가르치다	taught [tɔːt]
*think	생각하다	thought [θɔːt]

7 A – B – B 원형의 자음 + ound

원형	뜻	과거
bind	묶다	bound [baund]
*find	발견하다	found [faund]

8 A – B – B 원형의 모음이 하나로 줄고 + t

원형	뜻	과거
creep	기다, 포복하다	crept [krept]
*feel	느끼다	felt
*keep	유지하다	kept
kneel [niːl]	무릎 꿇다, 굴복하다	knelt [nelt]
*leave	떠나다	left
*lose [luːz]	잃다	lost [lɔːst]
*sleep	자다	slept
sweep	쓸다	swept [swept]

9 A – B – B 원형의 모음이 하나로 줄어듦

원형	뜻	과거
feed	먹이다	fed [fed]
*meet	만나다	met [met]
shoot [ʃuːt]	쏘다	shot [ʃɑt]

10 A – B – B y를 i로 바꾸고 -d를 붙임

원형	뜻	과거
lay	두다	laid [leid]
*pay	지불하다	paid [peid]
*say	말하다	said [sed]

11 A – B – B 원형에서 모음만 바뀜

원형	뜻	과거
behold	~를 보다	beheld
bleed	피를 흘리다	bled
breed	기르다	bred
cling	달라붙다	clung
dig	파다	dug [dʌg]
fling	내던지다	flung
hang	걸다	hung
*hold	잡다, 손에 들다	held
lead	이끌다	led
shine	빛나다	shone [ʃoun]
*sit	앉다	sat [sæt]
spin	(실을) 잣다	spun [spʌn]
*stand	서다	stood [stud]
stick	찌르다	stuck
sting	쏘다	stung
strike	때리다	struck [strʌk]
*win	이기다	won [wʌn]
wind [waind]	감다	wound [waund]
withhold	보류하다	withheld

12 A – B – B 모음 변화, 끝에 -d 붙임

원형	뜻	과거
flee	도망치다	fled [fled]
*have, has	가지다	had
*hear [hiər]	듣다	heard [həːrd]
*make	만들다	made
*sell	팔다	sold
slide	미끄러지다	slid
*tell	말하다	told

13 A – B – B' 모음 변화, 과거형 + n

원형	뜻	과거
awake [əwéik]	깨다	awoke [əwóuk]
*bear [bɛər]	낳다	bore [bɔər]
bite	물다	bit [bit]
*break	깨뜨리다	broke [brouk]
*choose	고르다	chose [tʃouz]
*forget	잊다	forgot [fərɡát]
freeze	얼음이 얼다	froze [frouz]
*get	얻다	got [ɡɑt]
*hide	감추다	hid [hid]
*speak	말하다	spoke [spouk]
steal	훔치다	stole [stoul]
swear	맹세하다	swore [swɔər]
tear [tɛər]	찢다	tore [tɔər]
tread [tred]	걷다, 짓밟다	trod [trɑd]
wake	깨다	woke
*wear	입다	wore [wɔər]

14 A – B – C

원형	뜻	과거
*begin	시작하다	began [biɡǽn]
*drink	마시다	drank [dræŋk]
*fly	날다	flew [fluː]
lie	가로눕다	lay [lei]
cf. lie (규칙 변화)	거짓말하다	lied
*ring	울리다	rang [ræŋ]
shrink	줄어들다	shrank [ʃræŋk]
*sing	노래하다	sang [sæŋ]
sink	가라앉다	sank [sæŋk]
spring	튀다	sprang [spræŋ]
*swim	수영하다	swam [swæm]

15 조동사

원형	뜻	과거
*must	~해야 한다	(had to)
*can	~할 수 있다	could [cud]
*may	~해도 좋다	might [mait]
shall	~할 것이다	should [ʃud]
*will	~할 것이다	would [wud]

16 뜻에 따라 활용이 달라지는 불규칙 동사

원형	뜻	과거
bear	참다	bore
	낳다	bore
bid	명령하다	bade
	말하다	bid
hang	걸다	hung
	교수형에 처하다	hanged

17 혼동하기 쉬운 불규칙 동사와 규칙 동사

원형	뜻	과거
bind	묶다	bound [baund]
bound [baund]	되튀다	bounded
fall	떨어지다, 쓰러지다	fell
fell	쓰러뜨리다	felled
find	발견하다	found [faund]
found [faund]	세우다, 창립하다	founded
fly	날다	flew [fluː]
flow	흐르다	flowed
lie	눕다	lay
lay	눕히다, 낳다	laid
see	보다	saw
saw [sɔː]	톱질하다	sawed [sɔːd]
sew [sou]	바느질하다	sewed [soud]
sit	앉다	sat
set	두다	set
wind	감다	wound [waund]
wound [wuːnd]	상처를 입히다	wounded
welcome	환영하다	welcomed
overcome	이겨내다, 극복하다	overcame

MEMO

신영주

2급 외국어 정교사 자격증, UCSD TESOL 취득(국제영어교사 교육자격증, University of California)
(전) EBSi 온라인 강사, 대치 시대인재, 이강학원 강사
(현) 프라우드 세븐 어학원 원장, 리딩타운 원장
저서: 체크체크, 올백(천재교육), 투탑 영어(디딤돌), Grammar 콕, VOCA콕(꿈을담는틀), 중학 영문법 클리어(동아) 등 다수의 교재 공저

이건희

쥬기스(http://jugis.co.kr) 대표
저서: 맨처음 수능 시리즈 – 맨처음 수능 영문법, 맨처음 수능 영어(기본, 실력, 독해, 완성)
　　　내공 시리즈 – 내공 중학영문법, 내공 중학 영어구문, 내공 중학영어듣기 모의고사 20회
　　　체크체크(천재교육), Grammar In(비상교육) 외 다수
instagram@gunee27

최신개정판
내신**공**략 중학영문법 **1** 개념이해책

지은이 신영주, 이건희
펴낸이 정규도
펴낸곳 (주)다락원

개정판 1쇄 발행 2021년 3월 15일
개정판 6쇄 발행 2024년 11월 19일

편집 김민주, 서정아
디자인 구수정
조판 블랙엔화이트
영문 감수 Michael A. Putlack
삽화 김진용

다락원 경기도 파주시 문발로 211
내용문의: (02)736-2031 내선 532
구입문의: (02)736-2031 내선 250~252
Fax: (02)732-2037
출판등록 1977년 9월 16일 제406-2008-000007호

ISBN 978-89-277-0893-3 54740
　　　978-89-277-0888-9 54740(set)

http://www.darakwon.co.kr
다락원 홈페이지를 방문하시면 상세한 출판 정보와 함께 동영상 강좌, MP3 자료 등 다양한 어학 정보를 얻으실 수 있습니다.

내공 중학영문법

신유형과 고난도 서술형 문제로 중학영어 내신 완벽 대비

최신개정판

개념이해책

정답 및 해설

1

DARAKWON

내신공략

중학영문법

개념이해책 1

정답 및 해설

CHAPTER 01
인칭대명사와 동사

 01 인칭대명사와 be동사

Let's Check It Out
p. 13

A 1 mine   2 her
   3 your   4 it
   5 Andy's

B 1 am   2 are
   3 is   4 are
   5 is

C 1 am   2 is
   3 is   4 are
   5 are

D 1 am   2 you're
   3 is   4 she's
   5 is / it's   6 are
   7 they're   8 ×
   9 is / ×   10 are / ×

Ready for Exams
p. 14

1 ③   2 ⑤
3 ④
4 His kids are / beach

해설

1 첫 번째와 두 번째는 3인칭 단수이므로 is를 쓰고, 세 번째는 복수이므로 are를 쓴다.
2 ⑤는 주어가 복수이므로 are를 쓰며, 나머지는 주어가 3인칭 단수이므로 is를 쓴다.
3 This is는 줄여 쓰지 않는다.
4 he의 소유격은 his이고, 주어가 3인칭 복수이므로 be동사는 are를 쓴다.

 02 be동사의 부정문과 의문문

Let's Check It Out
p. 16

A 1 is not   2 isn't
   3 It's   4 am not
   5 You're not

B 1 You are not so lucky. 또는 You're not so lucky. 또는 You aren't so lucky.
   2 He is not a flight attendant. 또는 He's not a flight attendant. 또는 He isn't a flight attendant.
   3 They are not our patients. 또는 They're not our patients. 또는 They aren't our patients.
   4 Shao Cheng is not Chinese. 또는 Shao Cheng isn't Chinese.

C 1 Is he French?
   2 Is the movie boring?
   3 Are they fourteen years old?

D 1 it is
   2 they aren't 또는 they're not
   3 it is

Ready for Exams
p. 17

1 ③   2 ②
3 ③⑤
4 aren't 또는 are not
5 we are

해설

1 be동사의 부정은 be동사 뒤에 not을 붙인다.
2 주어가 she이므로 Is로 묻고, 부정의 대답은 isn't로 쓴다.
3 ③ Annie는 부르는 말이고 질문은 you한테 한 것이므로 Yes, I am.으로 답해야 한다. ⑤ 의문문의 주어가 복수이므로 No, they aren't.를 쓴다.
4 '거미는 곤충이 아니다'라는 말이 와야 하므로 are not을 쓴다.
5 students라고 한 것으로 보아 you는 단수가 아니라 복수이므로 I am이 아닌 we are로 답해야 한다.

03 일반동사 3인칭 단수 현재

Let's Check It Out
p. 19

A 1 play   2 wear
   3 watch   4 eat

B 1 comes   2 runs
   3 catches   4 goes
   5 passes   6 washes
   7 does   8 studies
   9 flies   10 fixes
   11 grows   12 enjoys
   13 dances   14 has

C 1 get   2 has
   3 cries   4 play
   5 do

Ready for Exams
p. 20

1 ⑤   2 ③
3 ③   4 stays at the hotel tonight
5 has

1 ⑤ do[wash] the dishes: 설거지하다 / 나머지는 play: (운동, 게임을) 하다, 놀다
2 We, They는 복수 주어이므로 동사원형을 쓰고, She는 3인칭 단수이므로 동사에 -s를 붙여 쓴다. (wear a uniform: 교복을 입다 / catch frogs: 개구리를 잡다 / sit next to me: 내 옆에 앉다)
3 ⓑ My grandma, ⓒ Her dad는 3인칭 단수이므로 gets와 works가 알맞다.
4 주어가 3인칭 복수형에서 단수형으로 바뀌었으므로 동사의 형태도 stay → stays로 바꾼다.
5 '가지고 있다, 먹다'의 뜻을 가진 have동사의 3인칭 단수 변화형 has가 알맞다.

04 일반동사의 부정문과 의문문

Let's Check It Out
p. 22

A
1 don't
2 doesn't
3 Do
4 Does
5 Does / have

B
1 does not make
2 does not teach
3 do not pay
4 do not like
5 does not walk

C
1 Do you listen to
2 어색한 곳 없음
3 Does the musical have
4 Does her aunt teach

D
1 Do / I do
2 No, she doesn't
3 Yes, we do
4 he doesn't
5 No, they don't

Ready for Exams
p. 23

1 ①
2 ①
3 ⑤
4 My mother doesn't like grapes.
5 Does he his homework? → Does he do his homework?

1 일반동사 like의 부정문은 「don't/doesn't+동사원형」이다.
2 don't로 시작한 부정문은 주어로 3인칭 단수가 올 수 없다.
3 ⓐ not → is not ⓒ isn't → doesn't ⓓ Do → Does ⓔ watches → watch
4 3인칭 단수 주어의 부정문은 「doesn't+동사원형」이다.
5 do his homework(숙제를 하다)의 의문문은 Does he do his homework?가 되어야 알맞다.

Review Test
p. 24

01 ④
02 ③
03 ①
04 ①③
05 ④
06 ④
07 ②
08 ④
09 ④
10 My baby brother cries all the time.
11 am → are
12 Are[are]
13 Mine → My / am → is
14 She is 14 years old / Her hobby is boxing (또는 Boxing is her hobby)
15 They are kind to me.
16 studys → studies
17 Does[does]
18 Do they agree with me?
19 (1) He doesn't do all the housework.
   (2) Does he do all the housework?
   (3) Yes, he does.
20 Do I look okay

01 His shoes는 3인칭 복수이므로 are를 써야 한다.
02 주어가 3인칭 단수이므로 is를 써야 한다.
03 • 주어가 you이므로 Are를 써야 한다.
   • 주어가 she(3인칭 단수)이므로 Is를 써야 한다.
04 주어가 3인칭 단수이므로 ①은 aren't 대신 isn't를, ③은 are 대신 is를 써야 한다.
05 She drinks milk every morning but doesn't eat [have] rice.로 영작할 수 있다.
06 ⓑ ⓒ ⓔ는 복수라 들어갈 수 없다.
07 ① → wash ③ → go ④ → comes ⑤ → plays
08 Do/Does로 물으면 「Yes/No, 주어+do/does (+not).」로 대답하고 주어는 대명사로 쓴다.
09 ⓐ exercise → exercises ⓒ writes → write
10 주어는 My baby brother이고 3인칭 단수이므로 cries all the time로 쓰면 된다. all the time은 '늘'이라는 뜻이다.
11 주어가 3인칭 복수이므로 are를 쓴다.
12 you와 복수 주어에는 are를 쓴다.
13 '나의'는 mine이 아니라 my이며, 주어가 3인칭 단수이므로 is로 써야 한다.
14 여자이므로 인칭대명사 she와 her 그리고 이에 맞는 be동사 is를 이용한다.
15 동사가 is 아니면 are인데 주어가 될 수 있는 것은 I와 they이므로 주어를 they로 시작해서 쓰면 된다.
16 study의 3인칭 단수 현재형은 studies이다.
17 주어가 3인칭 단수이고 일반동사이므로 Does로 묻고 does로 답한다.
18 '그들이 나에게 동의한다고?'라고 되묻는 상황이다. 대화 속에는 agree, with, they, do가 있고 목적어는 '나'이므로 me로 써야 한다.
19 주어진 문장의 does는 본동사(~하다)이다. 따라서 doesn't 다음에 본동사의 동사원형을 써야 하므로 do를 써야 한다. 의문문도 마찬가지이다.
20 B의 응답으로 보아 Do ~로 물었으며, you라고 대답했으므로 주어는 I이다. 따라서 주어진 단어와 연결하여 질문을 완성하면 된다.

한눈에 쏙!

1 1) 너희들   2) 그것들
2 1) am not   2) aren't   3) 주어   4) Are   5) Is
   6) 대명사   7) it   8) they
3 1) comes   2) passes   3) studies   4) plays
   5) has   6) don't   7) doesn't   8) Do
   9) Does   10) 동사원형   11) do   12) does
   13) don't   14) doesn't

헷갈리지 말자!

1 This is
2 they're 또는 they are
3 deos → does / doesn't it → doesn't do it

해설

1 This is는 줄여 쓰지 않는다.
2 대답할 때는 대명사로 하며 those는 they로 받는다.
3 do의 3인칭 단수형은 does이다. / doesn't 다음에 동사원형을 써야 하므로 본동사 do를 넣어야 한다.

해설

1 '모음+y'로 끝나는 명사는 그냥 -s만 붙인다. (keies → keys)
2 pants는 a pair of로 나타낸다.
3 ⓒ piece of cheeses → pieces of cheese
   ⓓ many → much (또는 bread → pieces[loaves] of bread)
4 few는 '거의 없는'의 부정의 의미를 나타내며 friend의 복수형은 friends이다.
5 hand의 복수형은 hands, foot의 복수형은 feet이다.

---

06 부정관사와 정관사

Let's Check It Out   p. 32

A 1 ① a ② × ③ an   2 ① a ② × ③ an
   3 ① an ② × ③ a   4 ① × ② a ③ ×
   5 ① a ② × ③ an

B 1 The   2 the
   3 the   4 The
   5 The

C 1 ×   2 ×
   3 ×   4 the
   5 an

D 1 the   2 ×
   3 an   4 ×
   5 a

Ready for Exams   p. 33

1 ③   2 ③
3 ③④⑤
4 (1) on foot
   (2) by bus

해설

1 water는 셀 수 없는 명사로 부정관사를 쓰지 않는다.
2 서로 무엇인지 알고 있으므로 정관사를 쓴다.
3 ③ the 삭제 ④ My a → My ⑤ an → a
4 '걸어서'는 on foot이며 'by+교통수단'에는 관사를 쓰지 않는다.

CHAPTER 02
명사, 관사, 대명사

05 명사의 종류와 수량 표현

Let's Check It Out   p. 29

A 1 ③   2 ②
   3 ①   4 ③
   5 ②

B 1 ② → beaches   2 ② → tomatoes
   3 ③ → geese   4 ① → toys

C 1 many   2 much
   3 a lot of   4 a few
   5 little

D 1 cups   2 slice
   3 bowl   4 pair
   5 bar

Ready for Exams   p. 30

1 ⑤   2 ③
3 ②   4 few friends
5 handes → hands / feets → feet

---

07 지시 · 재귀대명사, 비인칭 주어

Let's Check It Out   p. 35

A 1 This   2 those
   3 These   4 it
   5 they

B 1 herself   2 themselves
    3 myself   4 itself
    5 by

C 1 ≠   2 =
    3 =   4 =
    5 ≠

D 1 인칭대명사   2 비인칭 주어
    3 인칭대명사   4 비인칭 주어
    5 비인칭 주어

Ready for Exams
p. 36

1 ⑤   2 ⑤
3 ④⑤   4 him → himself
5 Is it / It is

해설

1 those로 물으면 they로 답하며, 내용상 부정의 답이 와야 한다.
2 ⑤는 강조적 용법, 나머지는 재귀적 용법이다.
3 ④와 ⑤는 인칭대명사이고, [보기]와 나머지는 비인칭 주어이다.
4 동사의 주어와 목적어가 같으면 재귀대명사를 쓴다.
5 요일을 나타내는 비인칭 주어를 사용해서 의문문과 평서문의 어순으로 쓰면 된다.

Review Test
p. 37

01 ②   02 ③⑤
03 ④   04 ③
05 ①   06 ④
07 ③   08 ②
09 ②   10 ⑤
11 ③   12 ②④
13 ①③   14 ③
15 ⑤   16 ②
17 ⓐ, ⓒ, ⓓ, ⓔ, ⓖ
18 Are those your babies?
19 two pairs of socks
20 little
21 geese / the
22 ⓑ a dinner → dinner
23 himself to them
24 A school → The[My] school / by the taxi → by taxi
25 My t eacher i s p retty.
26 ⓒ → The boy ⓓ → an elementary school student
    ⓔ → the girls ⓕ → university students

해설

01 foot의 복수는 feet이다.
02 students가 복수 명사이므로 ③과 ⑤가 들어갈 수 있다.
03 piece는 셀 수 있으므로 pieces로 써야 한다.
04 ⓑ friend → friends ⓒ a little → a few
05 help는 셀 수 없는 명사로 부정관사를 쓰지 않는다. 나머지는 모두 an이 들어간다.

06 ⓒ와 ⓕ는 재귀대명사의 강조적 용법으로 생략할 수 있다. 나머지는 재귀적 용법으로 생략할 수 없다.
07 식사명 앞에는 관사를 쓰지 않는다.
08 old but strong man에서 old가 모음이므로 빈칸에 적절하지 않다.
09 blouse는 plenty of가 왔기 때문에 복수로 써야 한다. (→ blouses)
10 ⑤는 인칭대명사이고 나머지는 비인칭 주어이다.
11 ③ honor는 모음이므로 a가 아니라 an이 필요하다. (→ She is an honor to her parents.) ① My phone is just a watch. ② I bought two bars of soap. ④ These women are not firefighters. ⑤ He has a few safes in his basement.
12 A good tree makes[produces] good fruit.로 영작 가능하다.
13 ① 셀 수 있는 명사(secrets)이므로 little → few ③ change(잔돈)는 셀 수 없는 명사이므로 many → much로 각각 고쳐야 한다.
14 주어가 복수이므로 have, 요리사는 셀 수 있으므로 many, plenty of, lots of 그리고 chef의 복수형은 chefs이다.
15 one-room[wʌn-ruːm]은 발음이 모음으로 시작하지 않는다. doesn't는 틀렸으나 don't로 고쳐야 한다.
16 [보기]와 ②는 강조적 용법이고 나머지는 재귀적 용법이다.
17 a few는 셀 수 있는 복수 명사 앞에 쓴다.
18 단수를 복수로 바꾸어 쓴 문장이다. that은 those로, baby는 babies로 쓰면 된다.
19 양말은 a pair of로 세며, 두 켤레이므로 two pairs of socks로 쓴다.
20 조건에 맞게 영작하면 She has little money in her pocket.이므로 세 번째 올 단어는 little이다.
21 goose의 복수형은 geese이고, 서로 알 수 있는 상황이므로 lake앞에는 the를 쓴다.
22 식사명 앞에는 관사를 쓰지 않는다. ⓒ의 앞의 New York은 도시이고 뒤의 New York은 주를 뜻한다.
23 introduce의 주어와 목적어가 같으므로 himself가 되고, to 다음에는 them을 쓰면 된다. (introduce A to B: A를 B에게 소개하다)
24 school은 앞서 말한 것을 다시 언급하므로 the 또는 소유격을 써야 한다. 'by+무관사+교통수단'이므로 the를 빼야 한다.
25 ⓑ, ⓒ, ⓓ, ⓕ가 틀렸으므로(ⓑ an → a ⓒ a → an ⓓ a 삭제 ⓕ the 삭제) 각각의 첫 글자는 M, T, I, P이다.
26 ⓒ와 ⓔ 앞서 언급한 명사를 다시 언급할 때는 the를 쓴다. ⓓ 셀 수 있는 단수 명사이면서 모음으로 시작하므로 an을 쓴다. ⓕ 복수형이므로 a를 빼야 한다.

시험 직전에 챙겨 보는 비법노트
p. 40

한눈에 쏙!

1 1) much   2) lots   3) plenty   4) few
   5) piece   6) pounds   7) loaves
2 1) an
3 1) 강조적   2) 불가능   3) 불가능
4 1) 시간   2) 요일   3) 명암   4) 거리   5) it

CHAPTER 03

시제

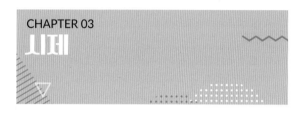

08 UNIT be동사의 과거형

Let's Check It Out   p. 43

A 1 was   2 was
   3 was   4 were
   5 was

B 1 wasn't   2 weren't
   3 wasn't   4 weren't
   5 wasn't

C 1 Were   2 Was it
   3 Was the mirror   4 Was your mother
   5 Were she and you

D 1 were
   2 were not 또는 weren't
   3 wasn't 또는 was not
   4 Were   5 was

Ready for Exams   p. 44

1 ③   2 ③
3 ③
4 ⓐ am → was ⓒ Were → Was
5 Gary and I were in the backseat

해설

1 ③은 was, 나머지는 were가 들어간다.
2 be동사 과거형의 부정문은 was not 또는 were not이다.
3 주어가 you이고 과거(last night)이므로 Were가 알맞다.
4 ⓐ 과거(last year)이므로 과거형으로 써야 한다. ⓒ 주어 (your new teacher)가 단수이므로 Was로 써야 한다.
5 that night으로 보아 과거임을 알 수 있고 and I가 붙어 있으므로 Gary and I가 주어고 복수이므로 were를 이용하면 된다.

09 UNIT 일반동사의 과거형

Let's Check It Out   p. 46

A 1 ① did ② had
   2 ① hit ② went
   3 ① ran ② tried
   4 ① saw ② caught

B 1 sold   2 visited
   3 read   4 made
   5 put

C 1 didn't skip   2 didn't wear
   3 didn't do

D 1 Did you drive   2 Did they like
   3 Did he pay

Ready for Exams   p. 47

1 ③   2 ①②
3 ⓐ spent → spend   4 caught / ate

해설

1 brush의 3인칭 단수 현재형은 brushes이고 과거형은 brushed이다.
2 ① didn't 다음에는 동사원형을 쓰므로 find로 써야 한다. ② 현재형이라 과거를 나타내는 부사구 last night과 어울리지 않는다.
3 「Did+주어」 다음에는 동사원형을 써야 한다.
4 과거(this morning)이므로 catch - caught, eat - ate로 쓴다.

10 UNIT 진행 시제

Let's Check It Out   p. 49

A 1 ① walking ② loving
   2 ① playing ② putting
   3 ① lying ② seeing
   4 ① running ② watching
   5 ① climbing ② shopping

B 1 is cooking   2 is doing
   3 isn't dancing   4 are laughing
   5 Are / having

C 1 was planning   2 was carrying
   3 weren't looking 4 wasn't smiling

D 1 are visiting
   2 wasn't[was not] eating
   3 Were you waiting

Ready for Exams
p. 50

1 ③   2 ②

3 ⑤

4 are / doing / am playing / smell / cooking

해설

1 swiming → swimming / sking → skiing / catchying → catching / helpping → helping

2 ① studing → studying ③ not having → am not having ④ plaing → playing ⑤ writeing → writing

3 첫 번째 빈칸은 Are, Were 모두 가능하나, 다음 빈칸의 선택지로 보아 과거임을 알 수 있다. 따라서 Were, wasn't, was가 맞다.

4 현재 일어나고 있는 상황에 대한 대화이므로 현재 진행형으로 나타내면 된다. 단, smell은 진행형으로 쓸 수 없으므로 현재형으로 쓴다.

Review Test
p. 51

01 ① ②   02 ②

03 ①   04 ⑤

05 ② ④ ⑤   06 ③

07 ③   08 ②

09 ③   10 ⑤

11 ② ④ ⑤   12 ① ⑤

13 ②   14 ②

15 ④   16 ⑤

17 The singer was not famous a few years ago.

18 I was not at home yesterday.

19 Are → Were

20 Your answer is C O R R E C T.

21 brings → brought

22 (1) They weren't[were not] the same price.
    (2) My niece didn't[did not] run a marathon.

23 Did[did]

24 ⓓ → were swimming ⓕ → became ⓖ → hurried

25 I am tying my shoelaces. / I was tying my shoelaces.

해설

01 주어가 3인칭 단수이므로 현재이면 is, 과거이면 was가 적절하다.

02 ②는 주어가 3인칭 단수라 Was가 와야 한다.

03 ② Were → Was ③ Was → Were ④ was → were ⑤ was → were

04 read의 과거형은 read이다. (형태는 같고 발음만 다르다.)

05 ① cought → caught ③ braught → brought

06 내용상 '여기 살지 않지만 방문 중이다'가 적절하므로 ③이 정답이다.

07 질문은 일반동사 과거형으로 해야 하며, 내용상 ③이 적절하다.

08 진행형으로 물으면 진행형으로 답해야 한다. (→ They are singing and dancing.)

09 • 주어가 3인칭 단수이고 현재형이므로 doesn't가 와야 한다.
    • 과거형이므로 didn't가 와야 한다.

10 ⓐ were slept → slept 또는 were sleeping ⓓ was → is (또는 now → then) ⓔ was having → had ⓔ에서 상태를 나타내는 동사는 진행형을 쓰지 않는다.

11 주어의 인칭과 수에 맞게 ② wasn't ④ weren't ⑤ Were 로 고쳐야 한다.

12 ① find의 과거형은 found이고 ⑤ '그녀의 것'은 hers이다.

13 B로 보아 3인칭 복수이면서 일반동사의 과거형 질문이어야 한다. ⑤는 내용상 옳지 않다.

14 cut에 -s가 없는 것으로 보아 과거형이다.

15 ④ Did 주어+동사원형이므로 taught이 아니라 teach가 필요하다. (→ Did she teach English at school?) ① He threw a ball to the wall. ② They had a beautiful garden. ③ I covered my eyes and cried. ⑤ My dad bought an expensive car.

16 sit의 -ing형은 sitting이다.

17 '과거에는 현재와 반대였다'는 내용이므로 be동사의 현재 시제를 과거형으로 바꾸고 부정문으로 만들면 된다.

18 부정문이면서 주어가 I이고 과거형이므로 wasn't 또는 was not을 쓰면 되는데 6단어로 써야 하므로 was not을 쓰면 된다.

19 과거(last year)이므로 Were로 물어야 한다. B의 답에서 we는 A의 you가 복수일 수 있기 때문에 맞다.

20 ⓑ만 was가 들어가고 나머지는 were가 들어간다. 과거 부사(ⓐ this morning ⓒ a few years ago ⓓ in the past ⓔ의 then)가 있는 것으로 보아 be동사의 현재형은 공통으로 들어가지 않는다.

21 과거(in the 15th century)이므로 동사를 과거형으로 써야 한다.

22 (1) be동사의 과거형의 부정문으로 weren't[were not]
    (2) 일반동사 과거형의 부정문은 「didn't[did not]+동사원형(run)」을 쓴다.

23 과거(yesterday)이고 일반동사(have)가 있으므로 Did로 묻고 did로 답한다.

24 ⓓ swim의 -ing형은 swimming이다. ⓕ 상태 동사는 진행형을 쓰지 않는다. ⓖ hurry의 과거형은 hurried이다.

25 현재 진행형, 과거 진행형으로 쓰면 된다. tie의 -ing형은 tying이다.

시험 직전에 챙겨 보는 비법노트
p. 54

한눈에 쏙!

1 1) was 2) was 3) 주어 4) No 5) weren't
   6) Were 7) were 8) were

2 1) moved 2) worried 3) planned 4) didn't
   5) 주어 6) 주어 7) didn't

3 1) -ing 2) -ing 3) not 4) -ing 5) 주어
   6) be동사

헷갈리지 말자!

1 was

2 weren't 또는 were not

3 did not come

해설

1 과거 부사구가 있으므로 be동사의 과거형을 쓴다.
2 No라고 대답했으므로 weren't 또는 were not으로 써야 한다.
3 일반동사의 부정문은 「did not+동사원형」이므로 came을 come으로 고쳐야 한다.

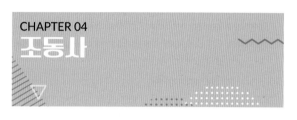

CHAPTER 04
조동사

UNIT 11 can, may

Let's Check It Out
p. 57

A 1 repair   2 can
    3 Can you   4 can't
    5 am

B 1 is able to   2 isn't able to
    3 Are you able to

C 1 허락   2 추측
    3 허락

D 1 can't   2 may not 또는 can't
    3 may

Ready for Exams
p. 58

1 ⑤   2 ⑤
3 ③
4 may not 또는 cannot[can't]
5 is → be

해설

1 ⑤는 허락을 묻는 '~해도 좋다'라는 뜻이고 나머지는 능력, 가능의 '~할 수 있다'라는 뜻이다.
2 can으로 시작하는 의문문이므로 can을 사용하여 긍정이면 「Yes, 주어+can.」, 부정이면 「No, 주어+can't.」로 대답한다. 단, 부정 의문문으로 우리말 뜻이 '응'이더라도 No로 대답한다는 점에 유의한다.
3 ⓐ mays → may ⓓ Do you can → Can you ⓔ plays → play
4 may not, cannot[can't]: ~하면 안 된다(허락의 부정)
5 조동사 may 다음에는 동사원형 be가 와야 한다.

UNIT 12 will, be going to

Let's Check It Out
p. 60

A 1 to visit   2 will
    3 listen   4 this evening
    5 be upset

B 1 Bora is not going to drink Sprite. (is not 대신 isn't도 가능)
    2 Is he going to invite us?
    3 Will you go camping tomorrow?
    4 They'll stay with you.

C 1 Yes, he is.   2 No, I won't.
    3 Yes, I was.

D 1 그 가수는 노래를 한 곡 더 부를 것이다.
    2 그들은 지금 공항으로 가고 있는 중이다.
    3 그는 곧 집으로 갈 것이다.

Ready for Exams
p. 61

1 ①   2 ④
3 ③
4 (1) is going to
    (2) is going to
5 she won't

해설

1 부사 soon으로 보아 미래 시제를 써야 한다.
2 조동사 will은 미래 부사와 함께 쓰일 수 있다. ago는 과거 시제에 쓰인다.
3 ⓒ late → be late ⓔ going → go
4 첫 번째는 현재 진행형(~로 가고 있는 중이다), 두 번째는 미래형(~로 갈 것이다)이다.
5 Will she ~?로 물을 때 부정의 대답은 No, she won't.로 한다.

UNIT 13 must, should

Let's Check It Out
p. 63

A 1 must   2 has to
    3 exercise   4 must not
    5 ought not to

B 1 Does he have to take the trash back home?
    2 We should reuse the water.
    3 Yes, you should.

C 1 의무   2 추측

D 1 must return home before midnight
    2 ought not to give up
    3 Does he have to take

Ready for Exams
p. 64

1 ②
2 ②
3 ①
4 ought not to
5 didn't have to

해설

1 그녀가 정말 필요하다고 했으므로 '우리 팀을 위해 경기해야 한다'는 의미가 되어야 한다.

2 ②는 '~임에 틀림없다'이고 나머지는 '~해야 한다'이다.

3 ⓐ not must → must not ⓑ to stop → stop ⓒ must → have to

4 should not은 '~하면 안 된다'는 충고·조언의 뜻으로 ought not to와 바꿔 쓸 수 있다.

5 '국경일이므로 학교에 갈 필요가 없었다.'가 알맞다. don't have to의 과거형은 didn't have to이다.

Review Test
p. 65

01 ②
02 ③
03 ③
04 ③
05 ②③⑤
06 ①
07 ⑤
08 ③
09 ⑤
10 ①
11 ①④⑤
12 ④
13 ③
14 ④
15 ③
16 ②
17 May
18 couldn't
19 ⓑ
20 90% → must be
　　50% → may[might] be
　　10% → cannot[can't] be
21 should
22 are not able
23 must[may] not
24 does he have to wear
25 Are we going to meet her?
26 don't have to

해설

01 ②는 '추측'이고 나머지는 '허락'이다.

02 be able to는 '~할 수 있다'의 의미로 can과 같은 뜻이다. may는 '~일지도 모른다'의 의미이다.

03 조동사 will 다음에 부정어 not이 온다. (→ will not meet)

04 must not: ~하면 안 된다 / don't have to: ~할 필요 없다

05 ① Do we must → Do we have to ④ don't have to → didn't have to

06 'Susan이 몸이 좋아 보이지 않는다'고 했으므로 '그녀가 아픈 것이 틀림없다'가 이어져야 자연스럽다. (must be: ~임에 틀림없다)

07 A가 should가 들어간 의문문이므로 대답에도 should가 들어간다.

08 내용상 도덕적 의무나 충고를 나타내므로 should를 사용한 ③이 적절하다.

09 last week는 과거를 나타내는 부사어로 미래형 부정어 won't[will not]과 함께 쓰일 수 없다.

10 ①은 '~해야 한다'의 의미이고 나머지는 '~임에 틀림없다'의 의미이다.

11 ① careful → be careful ④ to be → be ⑤ going → go로 써야 한다.

12 ⓐ, ⓒ, ⓔ가 옳은 문장이다. ⓑ doesn't has to → doesn't have to ⓓ working → work ⓕ yesterday → now (또는 Is → Was)

13 ③ 조동사 may 다음에 동사원형 go가 와야 알맞다. (→ You may not go first.) ① Can you ride an electric kickboard? ② Are you able to volunteer with him? ④ Do you have to finish the project? ⑤ We ought to save energy.

14 ⓑ ought to not → ought not to ⓔ don't have to → doesn't have to

15 ⓐ have to → has to ⓑ musts → must / late → be late

16 의미상 의무(~해야 하나?)로 물어보면 부정의 대답은 불필요(~할 필요 없다)가 자연스럽다. 금지(~하면 안 된다)는 어색하다.

17 '허락'(~해도 좋다)의 조동사로는 may와 can이 있다.

18 but으로 연결되었으므로 can의 부정형을 쓰고 before는 과거를 나타내는 부사이므로 과거 시제로 써야 한다.

19 should not과 ought not to는 '~하지 마라'라는 조언을 의미한다.

20 may[might] be(~일지도 모른다)는 약한 추측, must be(~임에 틀림없다)는 강한 추측이다. cannot[can't] be(~일 리가 없다)는 강한 부정의 추측이다.

21 그림에 please가 있으므로 강한 금지를 나타내는 must보다는 도덕적 의무, 충고, 조언을 나타내는 should가 적절하다.

22 can(~할 수 있다)은 be able to ~로 바꿔 쓸 수 있다. 이때 not은 be동사 뒤에 쓴다.

23 '금지'를 나타내는 must not 또는 may not이 알맞다.

24 「의문사+do/does+주어+have to+동사원형 ~?」의 순서로 의문사 의문문을 만든다.

25 미래 표현은 will과 be going to가 있는데 여기서는 go를 활용한 be going to 문장을 의문문으로 쓴다.

26 Do I have to ~?(의무)로 물어보는 질문에서 내용상 부정의 의미(불필요)가 자연스러우므로 don't have to(~ 할 필요 없다)가 알맞다.

시험 직전에 챙겨 보는 비법노트
p. 68

한눈에 쏙!

1 1) 동사원형
2 1) able　2) going　3) ~해야 한다　4) may not
　5) don't/doesn't have[need] to　6) not to
3 1) ~로 갈 것이다

헷갈리지 말자!

1 be able to 또는 삭제
2 Does

해설

1 조동사는 나란히 쓸 수 없어서 can을 같은 의미로 바꾸어 쓸 수 있는 표현으로 써야 한다.

2 have to는 일반동사이므로 의문문을 만들 때 3인칭 단수
를 주어로 하는 조동사 Does가 문장 맨 앞에 와야 한다.

14 의문사 의문문

Let's Check It Out
p. 71

A 1 Whose   2 Which
  3 Where   4 When
  5 Why

B 1 Who(m)   2 Which
  3 How

C 1 Whose   2 How
  3 When

D 1 What color is her phone case?
  2 Why did she leave early?
  3 Who moved my cheese?

Ready for Exams
p. 72

1 ⑤   2 ①
3 ④
4 What / mean
5 How

해설
1 의문사가 있는 의문문은 Yes/No로 대답하지 않으며 '무엇'
  에 관해 묻고 있으므로 ⑤가 적절하다.
2 각각 사람, 선택에 관해 묻고 있다.
3 What do you do?는 직업을 묻는 말이므로 운동을 한다
  (work out)는 대답은 적절하지 않다.
4 B의 대답으로 보아 사물(제스처의 의미)에 대하여 묻고 있으
  므로 의문사는 what이, 동사는 mean이 들어가야 함을 알
  수 있다.
5 각각 방법, 상태, 정도를 묻고 있으므로 How가 적절하다.

15 명령문

Let's Check It Out
p. 74

A 1 Don't   2 Cut
  3 Put   4 Never

B 1 Let's sing   2 Let's not waste
  3 Let's be

C 1 Fasten your seatbelt.
  2 Don't be too proud.
  3 Don't be angry.

D 1 hold   2 do
  3 Don't[Do not] 또는 Never (Let's not도 가능)
  4 join
  5 Let's not

Ready for Exams
p. 75

1 ⑤   2 ③
3 wash your hands
4 Do not touch.

해설
1 명령문은 동사원형으로 시작하며 내용상 be동사가 필요하다.
2 Let's 다음에는 동사원형을 쓰므로 took를 take로 써야 한
  다.
3 딸의 손이 더러운 것으로 보아 '손을 씻어라'의 명령문을 완성
  하면 된다.
4 Don't 대신 Do not을 써서 세 단어로 표현하면 된다.

16 부가의문문

Let's Check It Out
p. 77

A 1 are   2 wasn't
  3 didn't   4 can
  5 will

B 1 are you   2 doesn't he
  3 won't they   4 isn't she
  5 can he

C 1 aren't they   2 were you
  3 will she   4 will you
  5 shall we

D 1 wasn't it   2 didn't we
  3 will you   4 didn't he
  5 shall we

Ready for Exams
p. 78

1 ③
2 ③
3 ② ④ ⑤
4 (A) isn't she
  (B) No, she isn't 또는 No, she's not
5 He likes webtoons, doesn't he?

해설
1 be동사는 그대로 쓰고, 부가의문문이므로 주어는 대명사로
  쓴다.

2 명령문의 부가의문문은 will you이다.

3 ① 간접 명령문 (shall we → will you) ③ 「There+be동사」 구문에서 부가의문문의 주어는 there이다. (are they → are there)

4 (A) be동사의 부가의문문은 be동사를 그대로 쓰고 주어는 대명사로 쓴다.
(B) Mari는 의사이므로 부정의 대답으로 써야 한다.

5 앞 문장은 긍정의 평서문으로, 부가의문문은 부정으로 하면 된다.

ⓘ 17 감탄문

Let's Check It Out
p. 80

A 1 How 2 What
 3 How 4 What

B 1 What 2 How
 3 What 4 What

C 1 How large 2 How pleased
 3 What a strange girl
 4 What clean water

D 1 How → What 2 What → How
 3 a → 삭제 4 What → How

Ready for Exams
p. 81

1 ② 2 ⑤
3 ⑤
4 How excited the players were!

해설

1 형용사(scary)는 How로, 명사(building)는 What으로 감탄문을 만든다.

2 '웃긴 애'(funny kid), 즉 명사가 감탄의 대상이므로 「What (a/an)+형용사+명사 (+주어+동사)!」로 써야 한다.

3 computer가 단수 명사이므로 fast 앞에 관사 a를 써야 한다.

4 형용사(excited)가 감탄의 대상이므로 How로 시작하며 '주어+동사' 순으로 써야 한다.

Review Test
p. 82

01 ⑤ 02 ⑤
03 ② 04 ⑤
05 ④ 06 ④
07 ②③④⑤ 08 ③
09 Do not come again, will you?
10 What is your favorite subject?
11 How many teachers are there in your school?
12 ⓐ breaks → break
13 Put the gun down
14 won't you

15 wasn't she → didn't she
16 (1) will she
 (2) Yes, she will.
17 How fluently she speaks English!
18 그것은 참[정말로] 재미있는[흥미로운] 이야기구나!

해설

01 '시간'에 대해서 묻고 있으므로 ⑤가 적절하다.

02 좋아하는 색깔에 대해서 묻고 있는데 '빨간색은 나를 배고프게 한다'는 적절한 답변이 아니다.

03 Let's (not) 다음에는 동사원형이 온다.

04 일반동사가 있으면 be동사를 쓰지 않고, don't 다음에는 동사원형을 쓴다.

05 ① → is it ② → doesn't she ③ → can't she
 ⑤ → shall we?

06 • Let me ~는 간접 명령문이므로 will you를 쓴다.
 • 일반동사의 과거이고 주어는 대명사로 써야 하므로 did she로 쓴다.

07 ② → How big your son is! ③ → How clever she is! ④ → What a wonderful world it is!
 ⑤ → What a comfortable bed they have! (또는 What comfortable beds they have!)

08 ⓐ a 삭제 ⓒ How → What ⓔ a → an

09 명령문의 부가의문문은 will you이다.

10 '좋아하는 과목이 무엇이니?'라고 물어보면 되는데, 대답에 쓰인 단어를 2개 이상 사용해야 하므로 What subject do you like best[most]?는 답이 될 수 없다.

11 「How+형용사/부사」를 먼저 쓰고, 의문문이므로 「be동사+주어 ~」 순으로 쓰면 된다.

12 부정 명령문은 Don't 다음에 동사원형을 쓴다.

13 명령문은 동사원형으로 시작하고, put ~ down으로 쓰여 있으므로 the gun을 사이에 넣는다.

14 조동사는 그대로 쓰면서 줄임말의 부정형으로 쓴다. McClane은 부르는 말이므로 부가의문문의 주어를 he로 쓰면 안 된다.

15 과거형 일반동사(threw)가 왔으므로 wasn't가 아닌 didn't로 써야 한다.

16 조동사 won't가 있으므로 will she로, 부정의 '온다'는 내용으로 영어로는 긍정의 답변을 써야 한다.

17 부사(fluently)가 있으므로 How로 감탄문을 만들어야 한다.

18 감탄문에서 What은 '참[정말로] ~하구나'로 해석한다.

시험 직전에 챙겨 보는 비법노트
p. 84

> **한눈에 쏙!**
>
> 1 1) 주어 2) does 3) did 4) 동사원형
> 2 1) 동사원형 2) 동사원형 3) Let's 4) 동사원형
> 5) not 6) 동사원형
> 3 1) 주어 2) 조동사 3) didn't 4) 주어 5) does
> 6) 주어 7) will you 8) shall we
> 4 1) 형용사 2) 명사 3) 형용사 4) 부사
>
> **헷갈리지 말자!**
>
> 1 be → 삭제
> 2 a → 삭제

1 일반동사 come이 있으므로 be를 삭제해야 한다.
2 주어가 they이므로 fish는 복수이다. 따라서 a를 지워야 한다.

CHAPTER 06
형용사와 부사

18 형용사

Let's Check It Out
p. 87

A 1 =   2 ≠
   3 ≠   4 ≠
   5 =

B 1 many 또는 a lot of, lots of, plenty of
   2 much 또는 a lot of, lots of, plenty of
   3 a lot of 또는 lots of, plenty of
   4 a few   5 little

C 1 any   2 some
   3 any   4 some
   5 some

D 1 first   2 second
   3 ninth   4 eleventh
   5 thirtieth

Ready for Exams
p. 88

1 ②④   2 ③④
3 My cousin never spends any money.
4 few → (a) little / lot of → a lot of[lots of, plenty of, many]

1 • comic books가 복수 명사이므로 many[a lot of, lots of]가 알맞다.
   • 가격을 묻는 것이므로 How much를 써야 한다.
2 ③ cold something → something cold ④ five → fifth ⑤ opinion이 개인의 의견을 의미할 때는 셀 수 있는 명사이다.
3 never가 들어가면 부정문이므로 any를 써야 한다.
4 water는 셀 수 없는 명사이므로 (a) little이고, 셀 수 있는 명사의 '많은'은 a lot of[lots of, plenty of, many]로 써야 한다.

19 부사

Let's Check It Out
p. 90

A 1 quick   2 slowly
   3 carefully   4 happy
   5 really

B 1 ≠   2 =
   3 =   4 ≠
   5 =

C 1 well   2 too
   3 hard
   4 Lately 또는 Recently

D 1 She (V) talks to her ex-boyfriend.
   2 The twins are (V) late for class.
   3 (V) My mom and I (V) go shopping(V).
   4 What do you (V) eat for lunch?

Ready for Exams
p. 91

1 ①   2 ②
3 ⑤
4 What do you usually do after school?
5 balloons flew high

1 friend(명사) – friendly(형용사)의 관계이다.
2 동사(dances)를 꾸며야 하므로 형용사(good)가 아니라 부사(well)가 필요하다.
3 의문문일 경우 빈도부사는 주어 뒤에 온다. (→ Do you usually ~?)
4 의문문 어순으로 쓰되 빈도부사(usually)는 의문문이므로 주어 뒤에 쓴다.
5 그림에 열기구가 세 개이므로 단수인 balloon은 안 되고, flies는 주어가 3인칭 단수여야 하므로 부적절하고, '높이'라는 뜻의 부사가 필요하므로 high를 써야 한다. highly는 '매우'라는 뜻으로 적절하지 않다.

Review Test
p. 92

01 ⑤   02 ③
03 ②   04 ②④
05 ④   06 ②
07 ②⑤   08 ③
09 Wolves don't usually attack people.
10 I was pretty tired.
11 Too much pride is not good for you.
12 some special plans → any special plans
13 hard, ⓑ
14 The wizard had plenty of marbles.
15 twenty-one → twenty-first
16 humorously
17 not my type either

01 ⑤는 형용사가 명사를 간접적으로 꾸며주는 서술적 용법이고, 나머지는 직접적으로 꾸며주는 한정적 용법이다.

02 복수 명사(grapes)이므로 much는 올 수 없다.

03 ⓑ Do usually you → Do you usually ⓓ walk often → often walk

04 ② 딸이 7명인 것이므로 seventh는 seven으로 고쳐야 한다. ④ 부정문에는 any를 쓴다.

05 something은 형용사가 뒤에서 꾸며준다.

06 긍정문에는 too, 부정문에는 either를 쓴다.

07 ① highly → high ③ hard → hardly ④ near → nearly

08 긍정문에는 some, 부정문에는 any을 쓴다.

09 빈도부사는 조동사나 be동사 뒤, 일반동사 앞에 온다.

10 형용사나 부사 앞에서 '꽤'란 뜻으로 쓸 수 있는 p로 시작하는 단어는 pretty이다.

11 much는 셀 수 없는 명사(pride) 앞에서 꾸며준다. too가 '너무'의 뜻일 때는 형용사나 부사 앞에 온다.

12 의문문에는 any를 쓴다.

13 ⓐ '어려운'(형용사) ⓑ '열심히'(부사) ⓒ '딱딱한'(형용사)

14 '많은'이란 뜻의 p가 들어가는 단어는 plenty of이고 marble은 복수로 써야 한다.

15 세기는 서수로 읽으며 21의 서수는 twenty-first이다.

16 동사(speaks)를 꾸미기 위해서는 부사의 형태로 바꿔야 한다.

17 부정문에서는 '역시'라는 의미로 문장 끝에 either를 쓴다.

시험 직전에 챙겨 보는 비법노트   p. 94

한눈에 쏙!

1 1) body   2) thing

2 1) second   2) third   3) fifth   4) ninth
   5) twelfth

3 1) 빨리   2) 열심히   3) late   4) lately
   5) 가까운; 가까이   6) 거의   7) high   8) 매우

4 1) always   2) usually   3) often
   4) sometimes   5) seldom   6) never

헷갈리지 말자!

1 someone strange / ninth

2 late

3 is everybody always

1 someone은 형용사가 뒤에서 수식한다. / nine의 서수는 ninth이다.

2 lately는 '최근에'란 뜻으로 '늦게'란 뜻의 late로 바꿔야 한다.

3 의문문에서 빈도부사는 주어 뒤에 온다.

CHAPTER 07
비교 구문

UNIT 20 비교 변화, 동등 비교

Let's Check It Out   p. 97

A 1 hotter / hottest
   2 better / best
   3 smarter / smartest
   4 larger / largest
   5 funnier / funniest
   6 more exciting / most exciting
   7 more quickly / most quickly

B 1 as   2 not as
   3 outs   4 many

C 1 as fast as Aeri
   2 as much TV as you
   3 as many words as I

D 1 as / as
   2 not as funny as
   3 as white as milk
   4 as carefully as I

Ready for Exams   p. 98

1 ②   2 ③
3 ②④⑤
4 as high as

1 good – better – best / helpful – more helpful – most helpful

2 as ~ as...를 빼면 Lisa is ~.이므로 부사가 들어가면 안 된다.

3 ② as not → not as ④ much → many ⑤ my uncle → my uncle's car

4 왼쪽 건물이 오른쪽 건물과 높이가 같으므로 동등 비교로 쓰면 된다.

UNIT 21 비교급

Let's Check It Out   p. 100

A 1 busier   2 more
   3 more diligent   4 cold
   5 much

B 1 bigger   2 more interesting

3 less   4 worse
5 more careful

C 1 more[less] popular 2 fast
 3 much[still, even, far, a lot]

D 1 slower than
 2 more interesting than
 3 much[still, even, far]
 4 less popular than

Ready for Exams

p. 101

1 ③   2 ②
3 ③
4 taller than / shorter than

해설

1 than이 있으므로 비교급을 써야 한다.
2 내가 Morris만큼 바쁘지 않다는 것은 Morris가 더 바쁘다는 것으로 ②가 적절하다.
3 very는 원급을 꾸며주므로 비교급 강조 부사로 고쳐야 한다.
4 키에 관한 비교 구문의 형식에 부정문을 사용하지 않고, tall과 short를 이용하면 된다.

UNIT 22 최상급

Let's Check It Out

p. 103

A 1 the tallest   2 highest
 3 of   4 sports

B 1 heaviest   2 youngest
 3 most diligent 4 most important
 5 last

C 1 the oldest   2 most boring
 3 the largest   4 fastest
 5 islands

D 1 the best   2 the most popular
 3 the prettiest of

Ready for Exams

p. 104

1 ③   2 ①③④⑤
3 ③④
4 Fried chicken is the most delicious food in the world.

해설

1 「the+최상급+in+집단」이므로 ③이 적절하다.
2 ① Shape Shift가 무료(free)이므로 맞는 설명이다.
 ③ Army of Darkness가 4.99달러로 셋 중에서 가장 비싸다.
 ④ Shape Shift는 Mr. Giggle만큼 인기가 있지 않다.
 ⑤ Mr. Giggle의 순위가 가장 높다.
3 ③ most quickest → quickest ④ animal → animals

Review Test

p. 105

01 ⑤   02 ③⑤
03 ②③   04 ③⑤
05 ③⑤   06 ⑤
07 ③   08 ③
09 ⑤   10 ⑤
11 ②   12 ③
13 ③   14 ④⑤
15 play soccer as well as Messi
16 ⓑ little → less
17 as old as
18 (1) older than
 (2) not as old as
19 Jaykeun is the most popular student in our class.
20 (1) Zinga is bigger than the others.
 (2) Zinga is the oldest (of the three).
21 You are a ⒈g⒈e⒈n⒈i⒈u⒈s⒈!
22 (1) heavy
 (2) tall
 (3) lightest

해설

01 ⓓ sunny – sunnier – sunniest ⓔ pretty – prettier – prettiest ⓕ foolish – more foolish – most foolish
02 모두 원급 동등 비교 표현으로 '빨간색 상자는 파란색 상자만큼 작지 않다' 또는 '파란색 상자는 빨간색 상자만큼 크지 않다'를 찾으면 된다.
03 '축구가 야구보다 덜 인기 있다'는 의미의 열등 비교 문장을 찾으면 된다.
04 My grades are much[still, even, far, a lot] worse than before.로 영작할 수 있다.
05 학생들이 좋아하는 과목은 과학 〉 수학 〉 영어 〉 국어 〉 역사 순이다.
06 「the+최상급+in+장소」로 쓰이므로 ⑤가 옳다.
07 strong의 최상급은 strongest이다.
08 ⓑ boy → boys ⓒ more 삭제 ⓓ most → best (또는 most famous 등)
09 Lily가 여동생만큼 수다스럽지 않다고 했으므로 여동생이 언니보다 더 수다스럽다.
10 tasty의 최상급은 tastiest이다. (→ the tastiest food)
11 Judy와 Nana 둘 다 정직하다는 것으로 ②가 적절하다.
12 열등 비교는 「less+원급」으로 쓴다.
13 ③ great의 최상급은 greatest이고 the를 붙인다. (Mr. Bong is the greatest movie director.) ① He runs most faster than me. (→ most 삭제) ② Is math the interestingest subject? (interestingest → most interesting) ④ Did they arrive more earlier than us? (→ more 삭제) ⑤ Tomorrow will be the hotter than today. (→ the 삭제)
14 ① best → better ② diligently → diligent ③ largest → larger

4 delicious의 최상급은 most delicious이고 장소 앞에는 전치사 in을 쓴다.

14

15 than을 쓰려면 비교급이 없고, good은 형용사라 어색하다.

16 than이 있으므로 little을 비교급으로 써야 한다.

17 이 집과 저 나무의 나이가 같으므로 동등 비교를 사용하면 된다.

18 (1)은 비교급이므로 older than을 쓴다.
   (2)는 원급이므로 「as+원급+as …」를 부정문으로 쓰면 된다.

19 popular의 최상급은 the most popular이고 '집단'에는 전치사 in을 쓴다.

20 나이는 미소 〈 푸리 〈 징가 순이고, 크기도 미소 〈 푸리 〈 징가 순이다.

21 ⓑ more older → older ⓓ most funniest → funniest
   ⓕ names → name

22 (1) 'Buffy는 Jenny만큼 무겁다.'이며 「as+원급+as …」
   이므로 원급 heavy를 쓴다.
   (2) less ~ than이 있고 Jenny가 Buffy보다 '~하지 않은 것'은 키이므로 tall이 알맞다.
   (3) the가 있으므로 최상급이며 Cindy가 셋 중 에서 '가장 ~한 것'은 몸무게이므로 lightest로 써야 한다.

시험 직전에 챙겨 보는 비법노트   p. 108

한눈에 쏙!

1 1) busier   2) busiest   3) fatter   4) fattest
   5) more important   6) most important
   7) well   8) better   9) best   10) bad   11) ill
   12) worst

2 1) 원급

3 1) than   2) still   3) even   4) far

4 1) of   2) 집단

헷갈리지 말자!

1 not as comfortable as

2 much bigger than

3 one of the happiest girls

해설

1 as ~ as를 빼고 보면 are의 보어가 되어야 하므로 형용사 comfortable로 고쳐야 한다.

2 big의 비교급은 more big이 아니라 bigger이다.

3 'one of the+최상급' 다음에는 복수 명사가 온다.

CHAPTER 08
to부정사

23 명사적 용법

Let's Check It Out   p. 111

A 1 buy   2 to the store

---

3 To teach   4 to her
5 to the wedding

B 1 전치사   2 부정사
   3 부정사   4 전치사

C 1 목적어   2 보어
   3 주어   4 목적어
   5 주어

D 1 what to say
   2 how to choose
   3 when to press the button
   4 how to swim.

Ready for Exams   p. 112

1 ①   2 ②
3 ⑤   4 how to

해설

1 ①은 to 다음에 명사(장소)가 와서 '~로'의 뜻(전치사)이고, 나머지는 to 다음에 동사원형이 와서 to부정사를 이룬다.

2 빈칸은 동사 wanted의 목적어에 해당하므로 명사적 용법의 to부정사로 완성하면 된다.

3 [보기]와 ⑤는 명사적 용법 중 목적어 역할을 한다.
   ① ④ 진주어 역할 ② 주어 역할 ③ 보어 역할

4 how to ride a bike: 자전거 타는 방법

24 형용사적 용법, 부사적 용법

Let's Check It Out   p. 114

A 1 먹을 것   2 볼
   3 살 집

B 1 no water to drink
   2 a pencil to write with

C 1 (나)   2 (가)
   3 (다)

D 1 so / that / can't   2 so / that / can
   3 too / to walk

Ready for Exams   p. 115

1 ① ②   2 ④
3 ④
4 She is smart enough to understand the story.

해설

1 ⓐ는 부사적 용법 중 원인이고 ⓑ는 명사적 용법으로 '마시기를'이라고 해석한다.

2 [보기], ④ 부사적 용법(목적) ① 명사적 용법(목적어 역할) ② 형용사적 용법 ③ 부사적 용법(원인) ⑤ 부사적 용법(결과)

3 to부정사의 부정은 to부정사 앞에 not이 와야 한다. (→ not to catch)

4 형용사+enough+to부정사: ~할 만큼 충분히 …하다

Review Test

p. 116

01 ②	02 ③
03 ①	04 ①
05 ④	06 ④
07 ⑤	08 ③

09 to eat fried chicken
10 It
11 It is fun to play the board game.
12 I went to the Han River to take a walk.
13 He needs something hot to drink.
14 where she should find the truth
15 to become[be]
16 We have too much homework to have time to play.
17 Your hair is healthy enough to color.
18 can't → couldn't

해설

01 ⓐ ⓑ ⓕ 'to+동사원형'의 to부정사 ⓒ ⓓ ⓔ '~로, ~에게'의 전치사

02 '숙제를 하는 것을'이라는 의미가 되려면 명사적 용법의 to부정사가 와야 한다.

03 how to use: 사용하는 방법

04 to부정사의 부정은 to부정사 앞에 not을 쓴다 (to not watch → not to watch)

05 ④는 명사적 용법이고 나머지는 형용사적 용법이다.

06 ④는 '~할'로 해석되는 형용사적 용법이고, 나머지는 '~ 하기를'로 해석되는 명사적 용법이다.

07 There is 구문과 to부정사의 형용사적 용법을 이용하여 Now, there is nothing to stop us. (또는 There is nothing to stop us now.)로 영작 가능하다.

08 ⓐ에서 to write → to write on이 되어야 한다는 철수의 설명이 맞고, ⓑ와 ⓒ는 올바른 문장이다.

09 want동사 다음에 to부정사를 써서 목적어 역할을 하는 명사적 용법이다.

10 뒤에 진주어 to hide 이하가 있으므로 가주어 It이 필요하다.

11 It ~ to... 진주어-가주어 용법으로, 「It is+형용사+to+동사원형 ~.」으로 표현한다.

12 부사적 용법의 to부정사(목적)이다. (나는 산책하기 위해 한강에 갔다.)

13 「대명사(something)+형용사(hot)+to부정사」의 순서이다.

14 '의문사+to부정사' = 「의문사+주어+should+동사원형」

15 부사적 용법 중 '결과'이다. (연아는 자라서 유명한 피겨 스케이트 선수가 되었다.)

16 「too+형용사/부사+to+동사원형」: 너무 ~해서 …할 수 없다 / time to play: 놀 시간

17 enough는 형용사/부사를 뒤에서 꾸며준다. color는 '염색하다'의 동사로도 쓰인다.

18 문장의 본동사(was)의 시제가 과거이므로 can도 과거 시제에 일치시켜 couldn't가 되어야 한다. (나는 너무 부끄러워서 고개를 들 수 없었다.)

시험 직전에 챙겨 보는 비법노트

p. 118

한눈에 쏙!

1 1) 동사원형
2 1) ~하는 것 2) 부사적 3) ~하기 위해
3 1) too 2) to 3) enough

헷갈리지 말자!

1 couldn't
2 not to use
3 sit on[in]
4 dark enough

해설

1 주절의 동사 was의 시제에 맞추어 과거 시제로 일치시켜야 한다.

2 to부정사의 부정은 'not+to부정사' 어순이 알맞다.

3 sit on[in] chairs라고 하므로 on[in]이 필요하다.

4 enough는 형용사나 부사를 뒤에서 수식한다.

CHAPTER 09
동명사

UNIT 25 동명사

Let's Check It Out
p. 121

A	1 Jogging		2 swimming	
	3 drawing		4 singing	
	5 running			

B	1 studying		2 drawing	
	3 traveling		4 changing	
	5 Skating			

C	1 =		2 ≠	
	3 =		4 ≠	
	5 =			

D 1 go swimming   2 feel like getting
  3 was busy texting
  4 look forward to doing
  5 spends an hour finishing

Ready for Exams
p. 122

1 ④   2 ②
3 ③④⑤
4 to prepare → preparing
5 (A) enjoys singing   (B) like dancing

16

1 like는 동명사 또는 to부정사를 목적어로 취하는데, 두 번째 문장에서 전치사(about)가 있으므로 공통으로 들어갈 수 있는 것은 동명사이다.

2 ②는 진행형으로 쓰인 현재분사이고, 나머지는 동명사이다.

3 ③ Tell → Telling[To tell] ④ to type → typing ⑤ go → to go

4 be busy+-ing 구문으로 preparing을 써야 한다.

5 enjoy는 동명사를 목적어로 취하고 like는 동명사와 to부정사 둘 다 가능하지만 (A)와 (B)를 같은 형태로 써야 하므로 모두 singing과 dancing으로 쓰면 된다.

UNIT 26 동명사와 to부정사

Let's Check It Out
p. 124

A
1 holding
2 to go
3 taking
4 selling
5 moving

B
1 playing
2 to go 또는 going
3 to go
4 driving
5 to move

C
1 어색한 곳 없음
2 to take 또는 taking
3 listening
4 to travel
5 being

D
1 teaching
2 to ask
3 to lock
4 chatting
5 to teach

Ready for Exams
p. 125

1 ⑤
2 ④
3 ④
4 My (older) sister enjoys going rock-climbing.
5 stopped[quit, quitted] playing

1 want는 to부정사를 목적어로 취한다.

2 finish는 동명사를 목적어로 취한다. (to pack → packing)

3 I wanted to invite Kane, but I forgot to call him.으로 영작할 수 있다. forget to ~: ~할 것을 잊다

4 enjoy는 동명사를 목적어로 취하고, go+-ing는 '~하러 가다'이다.

5 stop+-ing는 '~하던 것을 멈추다'이며 stop의 과거형은 stopped이다. stop 대신 quit을 쓸 수도 있다. quit의 과거형은 quit 또는 quitted이다.

Review Test
p. 126

01 ⑤
02 ② ⑤
03 ③
04 ④
05 ⑤
06 ⑤

07 ②
08 ④
09 (1) 목적어
   (2) 넌 그 지붕 칠하는 것을 끝냈니?
10 speaking
11 is busy preparing
12 Have → Having 또는 To have
13 ⓐ having → to have
14 Much → Many / good → well / stop to try → stop trying
15 Everybody is tired of hearing her complaints.
16 to build → building
17 (A) lock (B) locking

01 전치사(for)의 목적어로 동명사를 써야 한다.

02 hate는 to부정사와 동명사를 모두 목적어로 취한다.

03 mind는 동명사를, hope는 to부정사를 목적어로 취한다.

04 'stop+to부정사'는 '~하기 위해 멈추다'이고 stop+-ing는 '~하고 있던 것을 멈추다'이다.

05 수영을 배우는 것(learning[to learn] to swim)이 주어이고, Learning[To learn] to swim is hard.의 의문문을 찾으면 된다.

06 ⑤는 현재분사이고 나머지는 동명사이다.

07 look forward to+-ing의 형식으로 쓴다.

08 ⓐ at 삭제 ⓓ to have → having

09 painting은 finish의 목적어로 쓰였다.

10 전치사 다음에는 동명사를 쓰므로 speaking으로 써야 한다.

11 be busy+-ing 형태로 쓴다.

12 동사원형은 문장의 주어가 될 수 없으므로 Have를 동명사나 to부정사 형태로 고쳐야 한다.

13 would like는 like와는 달리 to부정사만을 목적어로 취한다.

14 people이 셀 수 있는 명사이므로 many를 쓴다. / '잘'이라는 의미로 동사(know)를 꾸며주는 부사(well)가 필요하다. / '~하는 것을 멈추다'는 stop+-ing이다. (많은 사람들은 그들의 친구들을 아주 잘 알고 있다고 생각한다. 그래서 그들은 우정을 지키려고 노력하기를 멈춘다.)

15 주어가 Everybody이므로 단수 동사를 쓰고, of가 전치사이므로 hear는 동명사로 쓰면 된다.

16 「spend+목적어+-ing」 구문으로 to부정사를 -ing로 고쳐야 한다.

17 도둑이 든 상황으로 여자는 남자에게 문을 잠갔느냐고(lock) 묻고 있고, 남자는 문을 잠근 것(locking)을 확실히 기억한다고 대답하고 있다.

시험 직전에 챙겨 보는 비법노트
p. 128

한눈에 쏙!

1 1) 보어   2) 목적어   3) -ing

2 1) enjoy   2) mind   3) give up   4) finish
  5) practice   6) want   7) wish   8) hope
  9) expect   10) plan   11) promise   12) start
  13) begin   14) like   15) love   16) continue
  17) hate

3 1) forget   2) remember   3) try   4) stop

헷갈리지 말자!

1 meeting
2 making
3 to pick

해설

1 look forward to+-ing는 '고대하다'라는 의미의 관용 표현이다.
2 finish는 동명사를 목적어로 취한다.
3 그림을 보면 버스가 아이들을 태우기 위해 멈춘 것으로 'stop+to부정사'가 와야 한다.

CHAPTER 10
문장의 형식

UNIT 27 there is 구문, 감각동사(2형식)

Let's Check It Out
p. 131

A
1 is   2 Are
3 is   4 are
5 is   6 were

B
1 There isn't   2 Are there
3 There was

C
1 sad   2 good
3 smells like   4 tastes like
5 happy

D
1 tastes   2 like
3 soft[gentle]   4 feel like

Ready for Exams
p. 132

1 ① ④   2 ④
3 ⑤   4 ③

해설

1 ⓐ hot springs가 복수이므로 There are가 되어야 한다.
  ⓓ hope(희망)는 단수 취급하므로 There wasn't가 되어야 한다.
2 토끼는 한 마리이므로 There is a rabbit ~이 되어야 한다.
3 감각동사 sound 뒤에는 보어로 형용사가 온다. 부사는 올 수 없다. (loudly → loud)
4 ③ 'sound like+명사'이므로 like가 필요하다. (→ It sounds like a perfect plan.) ① Does it smell bad? ② He looks really tired. ④ The blanket feels so good. ⑤ The grape didn't taste sweet.

UNIT 28 수여동사(4형식), 사역동사(5형식)

Let's Check It Out
p. 134

A
1 him   2 Jane a letter
3 it to him   4 happy
5 to speak

B
1 to   2 to
3 for   4 of

C
1 to   2 for
3 to   4 for
5 of

D
1 sleepy   2 어색한 곳 없음
3 to stay   4 어색한 곳 없음
5 to marry

Ready for Exams
p. 135

1 ④   2 ① ⑤
3 ④
4 The groom gives the bride a ring.

해설

1 make는 목적격 보어로 형용사를 취하므로 uncomfortable로 고쳐야 한다.
2 name은 명사를 목적격 보어로 취한다. allow와 advise는 목적격 보어로 to부정사를 취한다.
3 간접 목적어 앞에 to가 있으므로 for를 취하는 get 동사는 올 수 없다.
4 신랑(a groom)이 신부(a bride)에게 반지를 주고 있으므로 「수여동사(gives)+간접 목적어+직접 목적어」의 순서가 알맞다.

Review Test
p. 136

01 ④   02 ④
03 ②   04 ② ③
05 ④ ⑤   06 ① ② ③ ⑤
07 ④   08 ③ ④
09 Is there any interesting news in the newspaper?
10 like
11 looks sleepy
12 a necklace for me
13 I'd like to cook *kimbap* for you.
14 *Songpyeon* looks like a half moon.
15 Who taught you to read and write?
16 My grandfather bought me a watch. (또는 My grandfather bought a watch for me.)
17 make
18 be → to be

해설

01 are there ~?로 물어봤고 five boats가 복수이므로 there are로 답한다.

18

02 주어가 many[lots of] cars로 복수 명사인 과거 시제 의문문이므로 Were there로 시작하는 것이 알맞다.

03 taste는 형용사를 보어로 취한다. (deliciously → delicious)

04 ② 감각동사 다음에 명사가 올 때에는 「감각동사＋like＋명사」의 형태를 취한다. ③ 감각동사는 보어로 형용사를 취한다.

05 ④ would like는 목적격 보어로 to부정사를 쓴다. ⑤ -thing으로 끝나는 단어는 형용사가 뒤에서 수식한다.

06 want, ask, tell, expect는 목적격 보어로 to부정사를 취한다.

07 gave는 4형식에서 3형식으로 바꿀 때 to를 쓰는 수여동사이다. 그러므로 ④는 Mom gave some advice to me.가 되어야 한다.

08 the poor(가난한 사람들)가 간접 목적어이고 some food(약간의 음식들)가 직접 목적어이다. give동사는 3형식에서 전치사로 to를 취한다.

09 news는 셀 수 없는 명사이므로 단수 취급한다.

10 a gentleman(명사형)이 왔으므로 like가 필요하다. 「look like＋명사」: ～같이 보이다

11 감각동사 look 다음에 형용사형 sleepy가 알맞다.

12 4형식 문장을 3형식으로 바꿀 때는 간접 목적어와 직접 목적어의 순서를 바꾸고, 간접 목적어 앞에 전치사를 넣는다. make동사는 전치사 for를 쓴다.

13 수여동사 cook은 3형식으로 바꿀 때 전치사 for를 간접 목적어 앞에 붙인다. would like to＋동사원형: ～하고 싶다

14 a half moon(반달)이 명사이므로 looks like가 알맞다.

15 Who가 의문사이자 주어이고, teach는 목적격 보어로 to부정사를 쓴다.

16 「주어＋동사＋간접 목적어＋직접 목적어」의 4형식 문장 또는 「주어＋동사＋직접 목적어＋전치사＋간접 목적어」의 3형식 문장으로 표현한다. buy는 전치사 for를 쓴다.

17 make는 4형식에서는 '만들어주다'의 의미이고, 3형식에서는 '만들다' 또는 '～이 되다'의 뜻으로 쓰인다. 주어가 복수이고 조동사 will 다음으로 make가 적절하다.

18 expect는 목적격 보어 자리에 동사가 올 경우 to부정사로 쓴다.

시험 직전에 챙겨 보는 비법노트　　　p. 138

한눈에 쏙!
1 1) 형용사
2 1) for　2) of
3 1) 형용사

헷갈리지 말자!
1 sad
2 for
3 to be

해설
1 감각동사 다음에는 형용사가 온다.
2 buy동사는 전치사 for가 온다.
3 expect는 to부정사를 목적격 보어로 취한다. (내가 너의 친구가 되기를 기대하지 마.)

CHAPTER 11
전치사와 접속사

29 시간 전치사, 장소 전치사

Let's Check It Out　　　p. 141

A
1	in	2	until
3	at	4	to
5	during	6	for
7	in	8	in

B
1	in	2	at
3	in	4	at
5	in	6	on

C
1	by	2	along
3	behind	4	under
5	through		

Ready for Exams　　　p. 142

1 ④　　　　　　　　2 ①
3 ⓐ ⓓ
4 a rainbow over the mountain
5 by 또는 beside

해설
1 짧은 시간이나 좁은 의미의 장소 전치사에 공통으로 쓰이는 것은 at이다.
2 on은 하루를 나타내는 날짜, 요일 앞에 온다. ① midnight(한밤중)은 짧은 시간의 의미로 at을 쓴다.
3 ⓐ in noon → at noon ⓓ 공항은 좁은 의미의 전치사 at을 쓴다. (on the airport → at the airport)
4 over는 표면에 접촉하지 않고 '～ 위에'라는 뜻이다.
5 next to = by = beside: ～ 옆에

30 등위 접속사, 종속 접속사

Let's Check It Out　　　p. 144

A
1	and	2	but
3	and	4	or
5	but		

B
1	so	2	because
3	If	4	so
5	if		

C
1	that	2	When
3	that	4	when
5	That	6	When

D 1 ⓒ   2 ⓐ
  3 ⓑ

Ready for Exams

p. 145

1 ①   2 ③
3 ②   4 That[that]
5 He studies hard because he will take a test
  tomorrow. 또는 He will take a test tomorrow, so
  he studies hard.

해설

1 '~한다면'의 조건을 나타내는 접속사 if가 적당하다. (일요일
  에 날씨가 좋으면, 나는 빨래를 할 것이다.)
2 ・「명령문 …, or ~」: …해라. 그렇지 않으면 ~할 것이다.
    (서둘러. 그렇지 않으면 너는 버스를 놓칠 거야.)
  ・or는 Japanese와 Chinese를 연결시켜준다. (그는 일본
    인이야, 아니면 중국인이야?)
3 ⓐ or → and ⓒ but → so[and] ⓓ because → so
4 각각 목적절과 주절을 이끄는 접속사 that이 필요하다.
5 '그는 열심히 공부한다.'와 '그는 내일 시험을 볼 것이다.'를
  because와 so를 써서 두 가지로 표현할 수 있다.

Review Test

p. 146

01 ②   02 ②
03 ②③⑤   04 ③
05 ①   06 ②
07 ③   08 ④
09 On   10 during → for
11 along   12 at / in
13 by   14 so
15 The sun is behind the cloud.
16 What / if / rains
17 but
18 when
19 If you come home early, you'll be able to watch
  the soap opera.

해설

01 요일 앞에는 on을 쓰고, 달이나 연도 앞에는 in을 쓴다.
02 특정 시점, 시각, 장소의 한 지점 앞에서는 전치사 at을 쓴다.
03 ② next → next to(~ 옆에) ③ 특정한 날 앞에 on을 쓴다.
   (in → on) ⑤ 거리 앞에 전치사 on을 쓴다. (in → on)
04 ③의 when은 '언제'라는 의미의 의문사이다. ①②④⑤의
   when은 모두 '~할 때'의 의미로 시간을 나타내는 접속사이다.
05 둘 중에서 선택하는 접속사는 or(또는, 혹은)이다.
06 강이 도시를 통과하여 흐르고 있으므로 전치사 through(~
   을 통과하여)를 써야 한다.
07 ・보어절을 이끄는 종속접속사 that이 필요하다. (사실은 그
    가 그것을 하지 않았다는 것이다.)
  ・목적절을 이끄는 종속접속사 that이 필요하다. (난 그녀가
    나의 의견에 동의할 것이라고 생각해.)
08 앞의 절과 뒤의 절을 연결하므로 접속사가 들어가야 한다. 뒤
   의 내용이 앞의 내용에 대한 원인이 되므로 이유의 접속사
   because가 적절하다.

09 특정한 날 앞에 전치사 on을 쓴다.
10 숫자로 표현된 시간 앞에는 for를 쓴다.
11 '~을 따라'라는 의미의 전치사는 along이다.
12 at the airport: 공항에서 / 도시 이름 앞에 in을 쓴다.
13 「on/in a+교통수단」 = 「by+교통수단」: ~을 타고
14 「결과+because+원인」 = 「원인, so+결과」 (너무 더웠기
   때문에 나는 에어컨을 켰다. = 매우 더웠다. 그래서 나는 에어
   컨을 켰다.)
15 '~ 뒤에'라는 의미의 전치사는 behind이다.
16 '무엇'에 해당하는 의문사 what과 '~한다면'에 해당하는 접
   속사 if를 넣고, 조건의 부사절에서는 현재형이 미래의 뜻을
   나타내므로 현재형 rains로 쓴다.
17 동해에 살지는 않지만 그곳에서 태어났다는 내용이므로 but
   이 알맞다.
18 '비가 올 때도 걱정하고 비가 오지 않을 때도 걱정하시네요.'
   라는 의미이므로 때를 나타내는 접속사 when이 알맞다.
19 내용상 조건을 나타내는 접속사 if와 뒤 문장의 주어 you를
   추가할 수 있다. (만약 네가 일찍 집에 오면 너는 드라마를 볼
   수 있을 것이다.)

시험 직전에 챙겨 보는 비법노트

p. 148

한눈에 쏙!

1 1) on
2 1) that   2) 목적어

헷갈리지 말자!

1 on
2 for
3 by taxi
4 arrives
5 is nice

해설

1 날짜를 나타낼 때는 전치사 on이 알맞다.
2 during은 특정 기간, for는 시간 명사가 온다.
3 'by+교통수단'에는 관사를 쓰지 않는다.
4 때를 나타내는 부사절에서는 현재형이 미래의 뜻을 나
   타낸다.
5 조건을 나타내는 부사절에서는 현재형이 미래의 뜻을
   나타낸다.

20

내공 ^신_략

중학영문법 **1** 개념이해책